Companioning the Grieving Child

A Soulful Guide for Caregivers

Also by Alan D. Wolfelt, Ph.D.

Companioning the Bereaved:
A Soulful Guide for Caregivers

Companioning the Dying: A Soulful Guide for Caregivers
by Greg Yoder   Foreword by Alan D. Wolfelt, Ph.D.

Companioning at a Time of Perinatal Loss: A Guide for Nurses, Physicians,
Social Workers and Chaplains in the Hospital Setting
by Jane Heustis & Marcia Meyer Jenkins   Foreword by Alan D. Wolfelt, Ph.D.

Understanding Your Grief: Ten Essential Touchstones
for Finding Hope and Healing Your Heart

Loving from the Outside In, Mourning from the Inside Out

Eight Critical Questions for Mourners: And the
Answers That Will Help You Heal

Healing Your Grieving Heart When Someone You Care About Has
Alzheimer's: 100 Practical Ideas for Families, Friends, and Caregivers

Companion Press is dedicated to the education and support of both the bereaved and
bereavement caregivers. We believe that those who companion the bereaved by walking
with them as they journey in grief have a wondrous opportunity: to help others
embrace and grow through grief—and to lead fuller, more deeply-lived lives themselves
because of this important ministry.

For a complete catalog and ordering information,
write or call or visit our website:

Companion
P R E S S

Companion Press
The Center for Loss and Life Transition
3735 Broken Bow Road
Fort Collins, CO 80526

(970) 226-6050   FAX 1-800-922-6051
drwolfelt@centerforloss.com   www.centerforloss.com

Companioning the Grieving Child

A Soulful Guide for Caregivers

Alan D. Wolfelt, Ph.D.

Companion Press is an imprint of the Center for Loss and Life Transition,
3735 Broken Bow Road, Fort Collins, Colorado 80526, (970) 226-6050,
www.centerforloss.com.

Companion Press books may be purchased in bulk for sales promotions,
premiums and fundraisers. Please contact the publisher at the above address
for more information.

Printed in Canada.

18 17 16 15 14 13 12   5 4 3 2 1

ISBN 978-1-617221-58-3

To all of the children, teens, adults, and families who have allowed me the privilege of "companioning" them out of the dark and into the light. You have been my teachers and encouraged me to inspire others to "bear witness" to families experiencing grief, loss, and the resulting transformation of life, living, and loving. What an honor to be able to attempt to touch the lives of people throughout North America and the world. Thank you! Thank you! Thank you!

CONTENTS

Preface

Please take pause for a moment to reflect on your own childhood losses and your struggles to understand your experiences with these losses. As you do so, I hope you recognize the need for resources intended to help adults artfully *companion* children in the journey into grief and mourning.

✳ ✳ ✳ ✳ ✳ ✳ ✳ ✳

To "companion" grieving children means to be an active participant in their healing. When you as a caregiver companion grieving children, you allow yourself to learn from their unique experiences. You let them teach you instead of the other way around. You make the commitment to walk with them as they journey through grief.

✳ ✳ ✳ ✳ ✳ ✳ ✳ ✳

It was in 1983 that I wrote the following: "Any child old enough to love is old enough to grieve." Since that time I've attempted to continue to learn from many grieving children and their families. I've also had the privilege of teaching and learning from thousands of caregivers to bereaved children throughout North America. I have certainly changed and, I like to think, grown both as a caregiver and as a human being in these last twenty-nine years.

On a personal level this growth is largely attributable to the births of my three lovely children, Megan, Christopher, and Jaimie. They, along with the children and adolescents I have companioned as a counselor, are my constant teachers. I hope the following pages reflect some maturity and wisdom gained over nearly three decades as a counselor. As I grow older, my inner child keeps reminding me that I must stay in touch with that little boy inside myself. Every day, even as my children are growing into young adults, they often remind me that play and good self-care should always be a priority in the journey of life and living.

Professionally, I am convinced that working with bereaved families, particularly children, is more *art* than *science*. I believe the current trend toward evidence-based research is inviting many caregivers to work with grieving families more from their heads than their hearts.

Each of us as caregivers to grieving kids must, in part, find our own way. We must combine our life experiences with knowledge, skill, and a creative, intuitive, flowing sense of joining the world of the hurting child. For me, counseling bereaved children is more of an intuitive, spiritual process than the traditional medical model of mental health care supports. I have left my clinical doctoring behind to become the grief gardener and "companion" that I am today, and I hope the grief gardening/ companioning model I offer in this book invites you on a similar journey of professional growth. ("What in the world is 'grief gardening'?" you're probably asking yourself right now. "Has Wolfelt finally lost it?" I assure you that I have not "lost it," but instead have gained much, personally and professionally, through the development of this model. But to understand what I mean by "grief gardening," you must read this book, particularly the parable on p. 5, the Introduction starting on p. 9; and the Tenets of Companioning the Bereaved on p. 12.)

✳ ✳ ✳ ✳ ✳ ✳ ✳ ✳

Bereavement literally means "to be torn apart" and "to have special needs."

✳ ✳ ✳ ✳ ✳ ✳ ✳ ✳

When I created this book in 1996 and now this most recent revision in 2012, I told myself I didn't want to add another academic textbook to the library shelves of educators and clinicians. While I must admit that I occasionally find myself thinking I should fill these pages with a multitude of research-based references, I have resisted the urge. I'm proud to be an academician-clinician and respect the need to draw on research in my work with bereaved children. However, I wanted this book to be about what I think and feel about companioning grieving children: what I do and how I do it. If this sounds interesting to you, please read on! If it doesn't, you may find other books more suited to your needs.

I have found that many people who work with grieving children are burdening themselves with thoughts that they should always know what to say and do. Many seem to want a cookbook, prescriptive approach to *treating* the child. I have found that the need to fill silences and treat bereaved children as patients results from contamination by a medical model of mental health caregiving. This model teaches us to study a body of knowledge, assess patients, and treat them with hopes of resolving issues and conflicts. In my experience, there is one major problem with this model as it applies to caring for grieving children—it doesn't work!

I realized years ago that the true expert in the counseling relationship is the bereaved child. This seems so obvious to me now, almost too elementary to write down. Yet this simple realization has proved profound to me in my work with children, teens, and families over the last three decades. Bereaved children are our finest teachers about grief and mourning. They are naturals! They don't play psychological games or hide out in efforts to repress genuine thoughts and feelings. They instinctively move toward it in natural doses, even when they fear the pain. As they mourn the death of someone loved, they tutor us in walking not behind them, not in front of them, but beside them. They know about the need to mourn; they just need safe places in which to do it in their own way and time.

If you work with grieving children, you will at times feel uncertain, even helpless. I don't always know why I'm responding the way I do when I'm with a grieving child; my reactions are never scripted. Usually I'm following the lead of the unique child. I like to say, "I invite children to the dance, but I allow and encourage them to lead." When I work with grieving kids, sometimes we actively embrace pain, but more often we laugh and have fun. Techniques I might use are merely in response to the evolving process. I want the child or teen to come to know me as someone who accepts and respects him for who he is and where he is in his grief journey (note my special chapter dedicated to teens). Not every moment is filled with some therapeutically profound insight, but I realize something is happening all the time. And, some of the deepest communication comes during our silences.

I remember being a child—at times a happy child, at times a sad or angry child. I remember feeling deeply (as I still do). I wondered about life and death. Sometimes I was scared and uncertain about my future and the future of my family. I loved to play with other children (I still do that, too.) I think my ability to remember my childhood provides me a view of children that children respond to. Yes, it's easier to be around children when they are happy. Yet we must also be present to them in their pain and loneliness. I hope this book helps you use your gifts to "be with" and learn from bereaved children and teens.

In recent years, my life has been touched by many losses. Both of my parents (Don and Virgene) died, my family home burned down just after Christmas 2009, and I had a health challenge that reminded me of my mortality. All of these losses have only left me more convinced of the value that I have to contribute to death education and counseling. I am at the same time humbled, yet proud, of what I do each and every day to help people mourn well so they can go on to live well and love well. With that said, I invite you to take what works from this book and leave the rest.

I hope we meet one day!

Alan D. Wolfelt

June, 2012

Prologue

<u>The Gardener and the Seedling</u>

A Parable

One spring morning a gardener noticed an unfamiliar seedling poking through the ground near the rocky, untended edge of his garden. He knelt to examine its first fragile leaves. Though he had cared for many others during his long life, the gardener was unsure what this new seedling was to become. Still, it looked forlorn and in need of his encouragement, so the gardener removed the largest stones near the seedling's tender stalk and bathed it in rainwater from his worn tin watering can.

In the coming days the gardener watched the seedling struggle to live and grow in its new, sometimes hostile home. When weeds threatened to choke the seedling, he dug them out, careful not to disturb the seedling's delicate roots. He spooned dark, rich compost around its base. One cold April night he even fashioned a special cover for the seedling from an old canning jar so that it would not freeze.

But the gardener also believed in the seedling's natural capacity to adapt and survive. He did not water it too frequently. He did not stimulate its growth with chemicals. Nor did he succumb to the urge to lift the seedling from its unfriendly setting and transplant it in the rich, sheltered center of the garden. Instead the gardener watched and waited.

Day by day the seedling grew taller, stronger. Its slender yet sturdy stalk reached for the heavens, and its blue-green leaves stretched to either side as if to welcome the gardener as he arrived each morning.

Soon a flower bud appeared atop the young plant's stem. Then one warm June afternoon the tightly wrapped, purple-blue petals unfurled, revealing a paler blue ring of petals inside and a tiny bouquet of yellow stamens at its center.

A columbine—the gentle wildflower whose name means "dovelike." A single, perfect columbine.

The gardener smiled. He knew then that the columbine would continue to grow and flourish, still needing his presence but no longer requiring the daily companionship it had during its tenuous early days.

The gardener crouched next to the lovely blossom and cupped its head in his rough palm. "Congratulations," he whispered to the columbine. "You have not only survived, you have grown beautiful and strong."

The gardener stood and turned to walk back to his gardening shed. Suddenly a gust of wind lifted his straw hat and as he bent to retrieve it, a small voice whispered back, "Without your help I could not have. Thank you."

The gardener looked up but no one was there. Just the blue columbine nodding happily in the breeze. . .

What It Means to To Be a Grief Gardener

When working with grieving children, I find it helpful to think of myself as a gardener tending fragile yet resilient seedlings and plants. With support, I help them grow through grief, letting them guide the journey to their own blossoming.

I am a grief gardener who companions children in their grief journey. Throughout this book, I reference gardening with hopes that you'll find this metaphor helpful in your work with grieving children. Another vital concept I use interchangeably with grief gardener throughout this book is "companion." It's my philosophy that as counselors we do not "treat" or "cure" our clients. Rather, we companion them on their path toward healing.

It is my hope that you will call on this parable to enter the frame of mind of a grief gardener. Unlike the medical model of bereavement care, in which grief is treated as a sickness that needs to be cured, grief gardeners believe that grief is organic. That grief is as natural as the setting of the sun and as elemental as gravity. To grief gardeners, grief is a complex but perfectly natural—and necessary—mixture of human emotions. Grief gardeners do not cure the grieving child; instead we create conditions that allow the bereaved child to mourn. Our work is more art than science, more heart than head. The grieving child is not our patient but instead our companion.

The seedling in the parable represents, of course, the bereaved child. The seedling is struggling to live in its new, hostile environment much as a grieving child struggles to cope with her new, scary world. A world without someone she loved very much. A world that does not understand the need to mourn. A world that does not compassionately support its bereaved.

This child needs the love and attention of caring adults if she is to heal and grow. It is the bereavement caregiver's role to create conditions that allow for such healing and growth. In the parable, the gardener removes stones near the seedling's tender stalk and offers it life-sustaining water. In the real world, the grief gardener might simply listen as the child talks or acts out her feelings of pain or sadness, in effect removing a heavy weight from her small shoulders. Instead of water, someone who companions offers his empathy, helping quench the child's thirst for companionship.

The gardener in the parable also dug out weeds that threatened to choke the young seedling; the grief gardener might attempt to squelch those who threaten the child's healing, such as a dysfunctional or grief-avoiding family member. Dispelling prevalent grief misconceptions (see Chapter One) is another weeding task for the grief gardener. The grief gardener's compost is the nourishment of play—that necessary work that feeds the souls of all children.

But notice, too, that the gardener in the parable does not take complete control of the seedling's existence, but rather trusts in the seedling's inner capacity to heal and grow. The gardener does not water the seedling too frequently; the grief gardener does not offer companionship to the point of codependency. The gardener does not use chemical fertilizers; he does not advocate the use of pharmaceuticals (unless made necessary by a medical condition, of course) or other inorganic therapies for grieving children. The gardener does not transplant the seedling but instead allows it to struggle where it has landed; the grief gardener does not seek to rescue the bereaved child from her pain.

Largely as a result of its own arduous work, the seedling in the parable grows into a beautiful columbine. Grieving children, with time and the loving companionship of adults, also have inside themselves the potential for this same kind of transformation. The greatest joy of grief gardening, in fact, is witnessing this growth and new beauty in bereaved children who have learned to reconcile their grief.

I invite you to keep the grief gardening parable and metaphor in mind not only as you read this book but also as you companion the precious grieving children in your care.

Grief Gardening Model Poster
A poster of this parable and an outline of my grief gardening model is available from my Companion Press bookstore. Visit www.centerforloss.com and click on Posters to select and order.

INTRODUCTION

A Grief Gardener's Guide to Companioning Grieving Children

I've always found it intriguing that the word "treat" comes from the Latin root word "tractare," which means "to drag." If we combine that with "patient," we can really get in trouble. "Patient" means "passive long-term sufferer," so if we treat patients, we drag passive, long-term sufferers. Simply stated, that's not very empowering.

On the other hand, the word "companion," when broken down into its original Latin roots, means "messmate": **com** for "with" and **pan** for "bread." Someone you would share a meal with, a friend, an equal. I have taken liberties with the noun "companion" and made it into the verb "companioning" because it so well captures the type of counseling relationship I support and advocate. That is the image of companioning—sitting at a table together, being present to one another, sharing, communing, abiding in the fellowship of hospitality.

The companioning model of grief care, which I created some years ago, is anchored in the "teach me" perspective. It is about learning and observing. In fact, the meaning of "observance" comes to us from ritual. It means not only to "watch out for" but also "to keep and honor," "to bear witness." The caregiver's awareness of this need to learn is the essence of true companioning.

Companioning the bereaved is not about assessing, analyzing, fixing, or resolving another's grief. Instead, it is about being totally present to the mourner, even being a temporary guardian of her soul.

If your desire is to support children in grief, you must create a "safe place" for them to embrace their feelings of profound loss. This safe place is a cleaned-out, compassionate heart. It is the open heart that allows you to be truly present to another human being's intimate pain.

When companioning children, it helps to use activities to create an atmosphere of play, which often stimulates sharing. In Chapter 5 you will find several techniques for counseling grieving children. For more activities, I also recommend *The Companioning the Grieving Child Curriculum Book: Activities to Help Children and Teens Heal* by Patricia Morrissey, available through my bookstore at centerforloss.com.

In sum, companioning is the art of bringing comfort to another by becoming familiar with her story. To companion the grieving person, therefore, is to break bread literally or figuratively, as well as listen to the story of the other. Of course this may well involve tears and sorrow and tends to involve a give-and-take of stories: I tell you my story and you tell me yours. It is a sharing in a deep and profound way. Of course, children often convey their stories through play (see Chapter 5) more than they do through words.

Finally, companioning is much different than traditional treatment. While treatment works to return the mourner to a prior state of balance (or an old normal), companioning emphasizes the transformative, life-changing experience of grief (the new normal). Treatment also attempts to control or stop distressful symptoms. Companioning, rather, demands observing and bearing witness. As companions, we are not experts who have the answers; we look to the bereaved child to teach us about his grief. We do not control his journey by creating a treatment plan; we simply show up with curiosity and a willingness to learn and listen.

Treatment vs. Companioning

Treatment Model	Companioning Model
To return the grieving child to a prior state of homeostatic balance ("old normal").	Emphasizes the transformative, life-changing experience of grief ("new normal").
Controls or stops distressful symptoms; distress is undesirable.	Observes, "watches out for," "bears witness." Sees value in soul-based symptoms of grief.
Follows a prescriptive model where the counselor is a perceived expert.	Bereaved child guides the journey; adopts "teach me" as the foundational principle.
A sustained relationship with the dead person is perceived as pathological.	A shift in the relationship from presence to memory is seen as normal and healthy.
Positions the grieving child in a passive role.	Recognizes the need for the grieving child to actively (in "doses") mourn.
Quality of care judged by how well grief was "managed."	Quality of care monitored by how well we allowed the grieving child to lead the way.
Denial interferes with efficient integration of the loss and must be overcome.	Denial helps sustain the integration of the loss from head to heart. It is matched with patience and compassion.
Assesses and creates a strategic plan of intervention.	Shows up with curiosity, willingness, and a desire to learn from the child. Honors the mystery; searches for meaning; doesn't feel need to solve or satisfy the dilemma.

❋❋❋❋❋❋❋❋❋❋❋❋❋❋❋❋❋❋❋❋❋❋

The Tenets of Companioning the Bereaved

Tenet One
Companioning is about being present to another person's pain; it is not about taking away the pain.

Tenet Two
Companioning is about going to the wilderness of the soul with another human being; it is not about thinking you are responsible for finding the way out.

Tenet Three
Companioning is about honoring the spirit; it is not about focusing on the intellect.

Tenet Four
Companioning is about listening with the heart; it is not about analyzing with the head.

Tenet Five
Companioning is about bearing witness to the struggles of others; it is not about judging or directing these struggles.

Tenet Six
Companioning is about walking alongside; it is not about leading.

Tenet Seven
Companioning means discovering the gifts of sacred silence; it does not mean filling up every moment with words.

Tenet Eight
Companioning is about being still; it is not about frantic movement forward.

Tenet Nine
Companioning is about respecting disorder and confusion; it is not about imposing order and logic.

Tenet Ten
Companioning is about learning from others; it is not about teaching them.

Tenet Eleven
Companioning is about compassionate curiosity; it is not about expertise.

❋❋❋❋❋❋❋❋❋❋❋❋❋❋❋❋❋❋❋❋❋❋

Why A "Soulful" Guide?

When I am in the presence of a grieving child, the soul is present. To look into the eyes of a child mourning the death of someone precious is to look into the window of the soul.

Children are especially soulful, for they have not yet worked on building walls around their true selves—the walls that hide their innermost thoughts and feelings. They are exquisitely transparent. Not until adolescence do the walls start to go up (which is why the grief of teens begins to become more complicated).

"Soul" is discovered in the quality of what I'm experiencing when I'm honored to be present to them. If my intent is anchored in truth and integrity, if they are discovering a reason to go on living (redefining their worldview and searching for meaning), then they are rich in soul, and so am I. Therefore, for me, companioning a child in grief means giving attention to those experiences that give my life, and the lives of those I attempt to help, a richness and depth of meaning.

Soul really has to do with a sense of the heart being touched by feelings. An open heart that is grieving is a "well of reception"; it is moved entirely by what it has perceived. Soul also has to do with the overall journey of life as a story, as a representation of deep inner meaning. Soul is not a thing but a dimension of experiencing life and living. I see soul as the primary essence of our true nature, our spirit self, or our life force.

Growth through Grief

Grief gardeners, or companions, provide a nurturing, gentle environment in which grieving children can not only heal, but grow. Like the columbine seedling in the parable, grieving kids can—after time and with the compassionate care of the adults in their lives—adapt to their new, sometimes hostile surroundings and go on to not just survive, but thrive.

Bereaved children can and do grow through grief. I have been privileged to witness this transformation many times. And when it happens, it is as jubilant, as exquisite, as awe-inspiringly *natural*, as the butterfly's crawl from the chrysalis or the tiny rosebud's explosion into bloom.

In fact, it is the potential for this type of growth that guides me in my work with grieving children. It is, at bottom, why I am a grief counselor. If I did not believe that grieving kids can heal and eventually flourish, I could not do the work I do.

But what precisely do I mean by growth through grief? I mean many things, the most important of which I will explore here:

Growth Means Change

My experience has taught me that we as human beings are forever changed by the death of someone we love. To talk about resolving someone's grief, which denotes a return to "the way things were" before the death, doesn't allow for the transformation I have both personally experienced and witnessed in others who have mourned. Mourning is not an end, but a beginning.

By using the concept of growth, I can go beyond the traditional medical model of bereavement care that teaches that the helping goal is to return the bereaved person to a homeostatic state of being. A return to inner balance doesn't reflect how I, or the children and families who have taught me about their grief journeys, are forever changed by the experience of bereavement. In using the word growth, I acknowledge the changes that mourning brings about.

Growth Means Encountering Pain

The role of suffering continues to be misunderstood in this culture. We seem to lack any understanding of how hurting is part of the journey on the way to healing. The painful yet normal thoughts and feelings that result from loss are typically seen as unnecessary and inappropriate. The grieving child who, because of his grief, has trouble with concentration is at risk for being mislabeled "attention deficit disordered." The bereaved child who tries to elicit caregiving through acting out is at risk for being mislabeled "undersocialized-aggressive behavior disordered."

"Buck-up therapy" messages in the face of pain are alive and well in North America. The messages we continue to give grieving children include, "You have to be strong for your mother," "You need to take care of your little brothers and sisters," or "Your grandpa wouldn't want you to cry." And combined with these messages is often an unstated but strong belief that "You have a right not to hurt. So do whatever is necessary to avoid it." In short, we continue to encourage bereaved families to deny, avoid or numb themselves to the pain of grief.

As our culture continues to avoid embracing the pain of grief, our children and teens are trying to get our attention. We must listen, learn, and respond in helpful ways. When grieving children internalize messages that encourage the repression, avoidance, denial, or numbing

✳ ✳

Children and Grief: Then and Now

In early American history, death was much more familiar to children than it is today. Because several generations of a family often lived in the same household, even very young children learned the naturalness of birth, aging, illness, and death.

Today's children have become one of the world's first "grief-free" generations. Modern medical discoveries have resulted in drastic reductions in infant and child mortality as well as prolonged life expectancy. As a result, the average American experiences a death in the family only once every twenty years. Plus, the much-discussed "mobility" of our society has scattered the extended family. And even when children and their grandparents remain in the same area, the increased use of hospitals and nursing homes—some of which have visitation policies excluding children—reduces the chances that children will witness the aging and dying of those they love and experience the normal grief that follows.

Our mourning-avoiding culture continues to make it hard for children to mourn in healthy ways, as well. Unfortunately we still believe that grief is shameful and should be "gotten over" as quickly as possible.

Still, those who adopt the companioning approach are working to make this world a more compassionate place for bereaved children. I have seen our successes in hospices, in schools, in special grief centers all across North America. If you haven't already, I hope you'll join us. It is my fervent hope that the children of the next century will mourn in healthy, life-giving ways with the help of caring adults—who are but children themselves right now. In helping today's bereaved child, we can leave a legacy of emotional and spiritual well-being for future generations.

✳ ✳

of grief, they may become powerless to help themselves heal. They may instead learn to act out their grief in destructive ways. Ultimately, not learning to "mourn well" results in not loving or living well.

But encountering the pain of loss all at once would overwhelm the child; therefore he or she must have a "safe place" for embracing pain in "doses." Sometimes bereaved children need to distract themselves from the pain of loss, while at other times they need a "safe harbor" to pull into and embrace the depth of the loss. (Obviously, this concept of valuing pain is contrary to the tenets of traditional medicine, which advocates the diminishing of pain.)

Growth Means A New Inner Balance With No End Points

While the grieving child may do the work of mourning to recapture in part some sense of inner balance, it is a new inner balance. My hope is that the term growth reflects the fact that children do not reach some end point in their grief journeys.

No one child, teen, or adult ever totally completes the mourning process. People who think you get over grief are often continually striving to "pull it all together," while at the same time they feel that something is missing. And adults who think people should "get over grief" will project this message onto the children they help. The paradox is that the more we as adults try to "resolve" a child's grief, the more the child will resist us.

A participant in one of my training seminars wrote me the following note upon her return home:

> *I know that in my own work of grief and mourning, I have always judged myself and secretly believed I was "wrong" for not being able to "resolve" my sense of loss and bring my various grief experiences to completion. . . . I continued to judge myself, to perceive myself as deficient or "less than." The concept of reconciliation freed me from the need to judge myself. It also permitted me to experience a remarkable sense of healing in my sense of "self" and in my belief in my ability to "handle" events in appropriate ways.*

This woman's experiences nicely illustrate how there is no end point to the grief journey—for people of any age, including children.

16

Growth Means Exploring Our Assumptions About Life

Those who companion are a philosophical bunch. Each time we meet a new grieving child, we tend to rethink the whys of human existence and, ever so slightly, amend our life philosophy so that it incorporates what we learn from this child. We open our souls to grief's lessons, much as the morning glory eagerly spreads its petals to the dawn.

Growth in grief is a lifelong process of exploring how death challenges us to examine our assumptions about life. When someone loved dies, we naturally question the meaning and purpose of life. Religious and spiritual values also come under scrutiny. Bereaved children may ask questions like, "If God is good, why did he make Mommy go away?" or simply, "Why do people have to die?"

Finding answers to these questions is an ongoing process for the grieving child. Indeed, children often don't form such philosophical beliefs until long into adulthood. Initially, we as caregivers can best help by not providing pat answers ("God knows best.") but instead allowing the bereaved child to explore his or her unique, appropriately childlike thoughts and feelings about life and death. I think it is lovely that children are so open to the mystery that naturally surrounds death. Now, ask yourself—can you stay open to a child being your teacher rather than perceiving it as the other way around?

Growth Means Actualizing Our Losses

The concept of "actualization" was first used in the counseling literature as it related to the growing process of an organism. The idea was then expanded on by such noted people as Abraham Maslow, Rollo May, Frederick Perl and Carl Rogers. As I will describe it in this book, the actualizing of loss emphasizes that experiencing and expressing one's potentials is essential to living.

The encounter of grief awakens us to the importance of utilizing our potentials—our capacities to mourn our losses openly and without shame, to be interpersonally effective in our relationships with others, and to continue to discover fulfillment in life, living, and loving. Rather than "dragging us down," loss often helps us grow. Loss seems to free the potential within. Then it becomes up to us as human beings to embrace and creatively express this potential.

In the garden, plants naturally grow to their fullest potential. If we provide them with the proper light, water, and nourishment, and tend to weeds and other pests, our horticultural charges will thrive.

Children, because of their straightforward optimism, also possess this innate tendency to flourish in a nurturing environment.

Still, not every grieving child or adult experiences actualizing growth. Unfortunately, some people do not seem to know how to grow or have conditions surrounding them that prevent such growth. They may remain emotionally, physically, and spiritually crippled for years. For children, this is strongly influenced by what the helping adults in their lives do or don't do to help them with their grief.

In fact, in our "mourning-avoiding" culture, more and more people are invited **not** to grow in their grief journeys. Our challenge as grief companions, then, is to fight this cultural tendency and instead extend bereaved children this invitation: teach me about your grief and let me help you discover how this experience can enrich your life. A large part of the art of companioning the grieving child is to free her to grow and live until she dies.

A not-so-secret hope of mine is that this growth-oriented, companioning model will eventually replace the medical model, which teaches that grief's goal is a movement from illness to normalcy. The growth model helps people understand the human need to mourn and discover how grief has forever changed them. It understands the normalcy of drowning in your grief before you tread water and that how only after treading water do you go on to swim. This growth model also frees helpers from thinking they have to "cure" a "sick patient." Instead, the helper is responsible for creating conditions that allow the bereaved child to actively do the work of mourning, dosing herself as needed.

Now you've read the principles that guide my work with grieving children. What are yours? I believe that every counselor must eventually develop his or her **own** theory about what helps bereaved children heal and grow. The effective counselor cannot and should not simply adopt the same ideas of another helper. Why not? Because she has not had the same life experiences and ways of perceiving and understanding the needs of grieving children.

I challenge you to write out your personal philosophy of counseling grieving children. You might start by asking yourself: What conditions do I believe help grieving children heal?

My Personal Tenets of Companioning Grieving Children

1. *It is my helping responsibility to create a safe environment for the grieving child to do the work of mourning.* (A bereaved child does not have an illness I need to cure.) I *collaboratively* work with the bereaved child. I do not assess, diagnose, or treat him. The traditional doctor-patient model of mental health care is grossly inadequate. Why? Because it creates expectations of external cures that involve the grieving child and family only minimally in the helping process. To be effective with bereaved children, I must see them as *active participants* in the work of mourning. I'm a caregiver, not a cure-giver!

2. *A grieving child's perception of his reality is his reality.* A "here and now" understanding of that reality allows me to be with children where they are, instead of trying to push them somewhere they are not. I will be a more effective helper if I remember to enter into a child's feelings without having a need to change those feelings.

3. *Each grieving child I meet is a unique human being.* A child's intellectual, emotional and spiritual development is highly complex and is shaped by many interrelated forces.

4. *While I believe children are able to experience feelings similar to adults', their thought processes are quite different.* A child's understanding of death depends upon his or her developmental level. As children mature, they may need to mourn in a new way based on these normal developmental changes. Therefore, helpers to bereaved children must stay available to help them for years after the event of the death. Mourning is a process, not an event.

5. *The relationship developed between counselor and child forms the foundation for all the work they will do together.* Empathy, warmth, and acceptance are essential qualities for the counselor working with grieving children.

6. *Play is the child's natural method of self-expression and communication.* To work effectively with bereaved children I must keep my own "inner child" alive and well.

7. *Bereaved children use behaviors (regressive behaviors, explosive emotions, etc.) to teach me about underlying needs (for security, trust, information, etc.).* I have a responsibility to learn what those underlying needs are and help the child get those needs met.

8. *Children are not only thinking, feeling, and doing beings, they are also spiritual beings.* Not everything we observe in children can be

precisely measured or construed. As a helper to bereaved children, I must remain open to the "mystery" that children keep alive in their young worlds.

9. *While the major focus in working with grieving children is on the present and future, I must encourage them to remember their past.* This historical approach aids in understanding the nature of the relationship with the person who died. It is in embracing memories of the person who died that the child discovers hope for a new tomorrow.

10. *While much of the grieving child's behavior and view of the world is determined by personal history and influences beyond her control, the growth process requires a hope for healing.* I have a responsibility to help the bereaved child not simply reach "homeostasis" but to discover how the death changes her in many different ways. As a growth-oriented grief companion, I work to help bereaved children not just survive, but learn how they are changed by this experience.

11. *I must work to create a social context that allows grieving children to mourn openly and honestly.* It is through this social context that the child can work on the six reconciliation needs of mourning.

12. *Some children do the work of mourning in the safety of a group experience.* The commonality of shared experience that comes from a support group provides a sense of belonging and helps normalize the grief process.

13. *While I am responsible for creating conditions for healing and growth in grieving children, the ultimate responsibility for healing lies within them.* I must remind myself to be responsible ***to*** bereaved children, not to be totally responsible ***for*** them.

14. *Right-brain methods of healing and growth (such as intuition) should be used more with grieving children than in the past and integrated with left-brain methods (intentional, problem-solving approach) if counseling bereaved children is to become more growth-oriented than historical mental health models of care.*

15. *The companioning approach to counseling grieving children sees children as possessing a wealth of strength, assets, and resources.* As I companion the bereaved child, I help her discover and make use of these strengths as she begins the lifelong process of mourning losses.

Companioning Basics: Essential qualities needed to companion children through grief

Those who companion children through grief have distinct traits. They are not only caring and loving, but are willing to let the child be the teacher. Here are key traits needed when companioning children:

Empathy

The foundation for accompanying a child through grief is empathy. To communicate empathy we must recognize and understand the inner experiences and feelings of the child *as the child experiences them*. This means we must develop the capacity to project ourselves into the child's world, to view the situation through the child's eyes—to understand the meaning of the child's experience instead of imposing meaning on that experience from the outside.

Don't think that empathy means passively waiting for the bereaved child to say something and then simply repeating what the child has just said. *Active empathy* means the caregiver is actively and attentively involved in a process of exploration. The helper tries to grasp what the grieving child feels inside. What is the inner flavor of this child's grief? What are the unique meanings of the death to that child? What is it that she is trying to express and can't quite say? What is her "play" trying to teach me?

Empathy involves expansion of one's boundaries to include the child. It is not identifying or losing oneself, but coming to know the child's experiences. To achieve this requires a here-and-now awareness of the thinking and feeling world of the child. It means being open not only to the content of what the child says, but also to nonverbal cues such as facial expression, tone of voice, gesture, and posture that reinforce (or at times contradict) the verbal messages.

While empathetic understanding is difficult in and of itself, it is not enough. We must also be able to *communicate* this sense of understanding to the child. The ability to communicate understanding helps children feel secure, trusting, warm, and affirmed. This quality of empathy frees children to explore any and all memories, both happy and sad. It is the essence of a companioning relationship.

- *Empathy means not trying to "fix things."*

    The more I allow the child to teach me, the less I find myself wanting to "fix things." Allowing myself to be taught seems to take the burden off me to get children where I would like them to go. The paradoxical aspect of this attitude is that the more I allow myself to be taught and follow the lead of the child, the more change and growth seems to occur. This is a very real part of my experience and probably one of the greatest gifts I have discovered in my life's work.

- *Empathy means creating a relationship.*

  Empathizing with a child also means making an effort to create a cooperative, hope-filled relationship in which there is a sense of working together toward mutual goals of healing grief's hurts. In many ways, this is the very foundation of a companioning model of compassionate grief care.

- *Empathy means being personally affected.*

  If you work to empathize with the mourner you, too will be open to the intense pain, fear, and deep sadness that is shared with you. The ability to empathize means a willingness to be involved in the emotional and spiritual suffering that is inherent in the work of grief.

A desire to understand

Closely related to active empathy is the desire to understand. To be effective in helping children cope with loss, grief gardeners must convey a commitment to understand. Communication—the sending and receiving of both overt and highly subtle messages—must occur between the adult and the child in order for understanding to take place. While we will not always understand the child's messages completely, the child will usually sense our ***desire and effort*** to understand.

Sensitivity and warmth

To companion, we convey sensitivity and warmth on many different levels. First, we physically demonstrate sensitivity by being aware of tone of voice, maintaining good eye contact, and staying cognizant of what is being communicated, both verbally and nonverbally.

Perhaps sensitivity is best described as an ability to sense what the child is thinking and feeling. Above all, sensitivity implies love, patience, and the ability to hear and respond to the child's needs.

Acceptance

When you accept the bereaved child, you consider him a unique, worthwhile person. To communicate acceptance, we must also remember that while children often ask questions that seem shocking or irrelevant to adults, we must respond to such questions without shock or embarrassment so that the child will feel loved and respected. We must also accept children not only for what they are, but also for what they are capable of becoming.

Genuineness

The child's grief companion must be truly herself—non-phony and non-defensive. Her words and behaviors should match her inner feelings. Genuineness creates safety for the child to do the work of mourning.

Trust

Grieving kids often feel a lack of trust in their world because of the death of someone loved. They often wonder if they should risk trusting or loving again. The bereaved child must learn, slowly and over time, that he can trust again. A trusting counseling relationship can become a bridge to the world at large for the grieving child. In large part, trust is about **consistency** and **safety**.

Spontaneity

You may have rarely, if ever, seen this characteristic noted in descriptions of core conditions of effective helping relationships. However, in working with children, I see this as vital! You might think of spontaneity as a facet of *intuition*. I find that the more I work with bereaved kids, the more I rely on my intuition as I respond to their words and behaviors instead of any set-in-stone clinical approach. I do and say what "feels right" rather than overanalyzing my every move.

The gift of spontaneity is that it creates a dynamic "here and now" experience for both the child and the counselor. Spontaneous ways of being in the relationship allow the child to use unique and creative ways of doing the work of mourning.

Humor

Humor is essential when working with children. Laughter lifts a child out of grief, if only for a moment, and allows feelings of hope, faith, and safety to enter. Humor is a great way to build rapport, especially with teens. Don't work too hard at humor; let it develop naturally from the conversation.

Flexibility

Flexibility is a close cousin to spontaneity. There is no "one way" for a counselor to counsel grieving children. I also want to reinforce that there is no right way for a specific counselor to work with all children, nor is there a fixed or static way for a counselor to work with a particular child. Flexibility means a willingness to change, to modify, to switch courses when such moments become appropriate. Flexibility, in part, means going on a mutual search to discover safe ways for the child to mourn in her own unique way.

A belief in the child's capacity to heal

In a companioning relationship, the counselor communicates her desire to "hang in there" with the child, to walk with her through her time of need, and to care beyond the confines of the professional work role. This kind of counselor commitment helps instill trust, self-respect, and hope for healing in the bereaved child.

The desire to be a "responsible rebel" and come from the heart

I believe truly helpful companions to children in pain are responsible rebels: They facilitate creative healing as they become fellow travelers in the child's journey. They do not function as agents of conformity to "get the child over" grief, but instead foster growth in the grieving child. They stay in touch with their hearts without becoming contaminated by the formality of professional training.

❊ ❊ ❊

In order to companion grieving kids, it's helpful to first clear misconceptions about grief from your mind. The next chapter reviews 10 common misconceptions about children's grief and mourning.

❊ ❊ ❊ ❊ ❊ ❊ ❊ ❊ ❊ ❊ ❊ ❊ ❊ ❊ ❊ ❊ ❊ ❊ ❊

Responsible Rebel: One who questions assumptive models surrounding grief and loss and challenges those very models. Rebels are not afraid to question established structures and forms. At the same time, rebels respect the rights of others to use different models of understanding, and provide leadership in ways that empower people rather than diminish them. So, if the contents of this book resonate with you, please join me in being a responsible rebel!

❊ ❊ ❊ ❊ ❊ ❊ ❊ ❊ ❊ ❊ ❊ ❊ ❊ ❊ ❊ ❊ ❊ ❊ ❊

Chapter One

10 Common Misconceptions about Grief

The following misconceptions may seem harmless, but I have found that when adults (and subsequently the children in their care) internalize them, they quickly become hurdles to healing. You might think of them as weeds in the grief garden. If they are allowed to grow unchecked, their aggressive habits will soon overtake the garden, choking out the impressionable seedlings.

As a fellow grief companion, I hope you'll join me in helping to dispel these misconceptions.

Grief Misconception #1

Grief and mourning are the same experience.

People tend to use the words "grief" and "mourning" interchangeably. However, there is an important distinction between the two—a distinction that becomes all the more critical for those who work with bereaved children.

Grief represents the thoughts and feelings that are experienced within children when someone they love dies. Grief is the internal meaning given to the experience of bereavement. *Mourning*, on the other hand, means taking the internal experience of grief and expressing it outside oneself. Another way to think of mourning is "grief gone public," or "sharing one's grief with others." Because grieving children mourn more through their behaviors than they do through words, mourning for them is not expressed in the same ways it is for adults.

When people actively grieve and mourn, there is movement. In other words, their emotions are in motion. The term "perturbation" refers to the capacity to experience change and movement. To integrate grief, children must be touched by what they experience. When they cannot feel a feeling, they are unable to be changed by it, and instead of perturbation, they become "stuck." When stuck, children carry their grief rather than release it, sometimes into adulthood. Yet when children actively mourn, they open their hearts to love and the feelings of loss. This openness welcomes a transformation of living and loving.

We often refer to children as "forgotten mourners." Why? Because though children grieve, we as a society often do not encourage them to mourn. As we companion, we have the responsibility and the privilege to create conditions in which children **can** mourn.

Grief Misconception #2

Children only grieve for a short time.

Many adults simply do not understand that grief and mourning are processes, not events. Those adults who want the bereaved child to "hurry up" and "get over it" usually project that the child needs to be strong and stoic. (Of course, who are these adults really protecting? Themselves. If adults can assume the child's grief and mourning are short in duration, then they don't have to walk with the child as he encounters the pain of loss.)

I have read in professional texts comments like, "If the child's symptoms persist past six months, he or she should be referred for professional assistance." Actually, nothing could be further from the truth. Around six months after a death, it is not unusual to see **more**, not fewer, visible signs of mourning in a child. This is largely because for children, grief gets intertwined with the developmental process. If I'm just five years old when I first come to grief, that grief will change for me as I mature and begin to understand it with more cognitive depth.

So how long should a child's grief last? If ideal conditions exist (which they rarely do) and the child is actively working on his six needs of mourning with the support of caring adults and family members, active mourning can still take three to four years. And even that lucky child will encounter intermittent mourning as he develops and reintegrates his grief experience. Remember—grief waits on welcome, not on time!

My best counsel is this: Keep in mind that grief does not have a definite end. Only as the child participates in authentic mourning will it erupt less frequently. Strive to be a long-term stabilizer in the child's life as he grows and develops. He will teach you that there will be some more natural times when he wants to do more "catch-up" mourning.

Grief Misconception #3

A child's grief proceeds in predictable, orderly stages.

Have you ever heard a well-meaning but misinformed someone say of a grieving child, "He's in stage two"? If only it were that simple! People use the "stages of grief" to try to make sense of an experience that isn't as orderly and predictable as we would like it to be.

The concept of "stages" was popularized in 1969 with the publication of Elizabeth Kübler-Ross' landmark text *On Death and Dying*. Kübler-Ross never intended that people should interpret her "five stages of dying" literally. However, many people have done just that, not only with the process of dying, but with the processes of bereavement, grief, and mourning as well.

No two children are alike. No two children will grieve and mourn in the same way. As caring adults, we only get ourselves in trouble when we try to prescribe what a child's grief and mourning experiences should be.

A good gardener doesn't approach his garden with textbook in hand and say, "Well, today I must water thoroughly and thin the new seedlings." Instead, he examines the garden on hands and knees and only then decides what is needed that day. Likewise, the grief gardener encourages the bereaved child to teach her about the child's needs: "Teach me about your grief, and I will be with you. As you teach me, I will follow the lead you provide and attempt to be a stabilizing and empathetic presence."

To think that one's goal is to move children through the stages of grief would be a misuse of counsel. Children experience a variety of unique thoughts, feelings, and behaviors as part of the healing process. We must remind ourselves not to prescribe how and when they should mourn, but allow them to teach us where they are in the process.

Grief Misconception #4

Infants and toddlers are too young to grieve and mourn.

In my experience, any child old enough to love is old enough to grieve and mourn. In fact, I see children as young as eighteen months old in my counseling center.

Infants and toddlers are certainly capable of giving and receiving love. While they cannot verbally teach us about their grief, they protest their losses in a variety of ways. A few practical examples are regressive behaviors, sleep disturbances, and explosive emotions. John Bowlby's research has shown us that even babies will protest when threatened with separation, death, or abandonment.

Unless we support and nurture infants and toddlers when they are confronted with the loss of a primary relationship, they can develop a lack of trust in the world around them. Holding, hugging, and playing with them are the primary ways in which we can attempt to help young children. We can also teach the parents of grieving infants and toddlers how best to care for them. For more on infant and toddler and grief, see the box starting on p. 42.

Grief Misconception #5

Parents don't have to mourn for their children to mourn.

My experience has taught me that parents and other significant adults in a child's life have the biggest influence on the child's own grief experiences. The problem comes when these parents, however loving and well-intentioned, try to conceal their own grief and mourning from their children in an attempt to protect them from more pain. This is a mistake. Modeling is a primary way in which children learn.

Children instinctively love and try to emulate their parents. So when the parents deny their own grief, they teach their children to do the very same thing. When Mom or Dad is openly sad, children learn that mourning is OK and that the sadness everyone is feeling is not their fault. Children who haven't been taught these things will often assume they are responsible for the emotional environment of the household.

One of the most loving things we can do as bereaved adults is allow ourselves to mourn; the first step in helping grieving children is to help ourselves. In fact, our ongoing ability to give and receive love **depends** on our willingness to mourn in healthy ways.

Grief Misconception #6

Grieving children grow to be maladjusted adults.

Grieving kids heal and grow with early support and compassionate care. Historical research may have us believe otherwise. Since the 1930s, numerous studies have attempted to establish relationships between childhood bereavement and later adult "mental illness" (depression, psychosis, sociopathic behavior). More recently, however, analyses of the research literature have questioned these results because of methodological problems with the studies.

Still people perpetuate this misconception. You may have witnessed this when adults approach bereaved children with this patronizing attitude: "You poor child. You will be forever maimed by this experience."

I repeat: Grieving children are not damaged goods. In my own experience, if adults create conditions that allow a child to mourn in healthy ways, there's no reason for the self-fulfilling prophecy that the child will be irreparably harmed by the death. I do agree that bereaved children are at *risk* for emotional problems, but only if they are not compassionately companioned in their grief journeys. If we create conditions that help children mourn well, they'll go on to live and love well.

Grief Misconception #7

Children are better off if they don't attend funerals.

Adults who have internalized this misconception create an environment that prematurely moves children away from grief and mourning. The funeral provides a structure that allows and encourages both adults and children to comfort each other, openly mourn, and honor the life of the person who has died.

Meaningful funerals form the foundation for healthy mourning just as properly prepared soil forms the foundation of a healthy garden. If we skip these crucial first steps, we fail to prepare adequately for the future.

Children, who after all are mourners too, should have the same opportunity to attend funerals as any other member of the family. They should be encouraged to attend, but never forced. I emphasize the word "encouraged" because some children are anxious when experiencing something unknown to them. Through gentle encouragement, loving adults can help grieving kids know they will be supported during this naturally sad and frightening time in their young lives. The funeral can even provide an opportunity for children to express their unique relationship with the person who has died by including

Helping Children with Funerals Brochure
This brochure, available through the Companion Press bookstore, gives families and caregivers helpful tips on companioning infants and toddlers through grief and mourning. Visit www.centerforloss.com and click on Brochures to select and order. This brochure is a part of The Helping Series which offers 35 brochures on different topics for easy distribution to clients and families.

a ritual of their own during the service. (For more on children and funerals, see p. 54.)

Grief Misconception #8

Children who cry too much are being weak and harming themselves in the long run.

Crying is the body's natural and cleansing response to sadness. It helps children release internal tensions and allows them to communicate a need to be comforted.

Children may repress their tears (and other emotional releases) either because they have internalized adult demands for repressing feelings, or they have observed that the adults around them repress their own tears. Unfortunately, many adults associate tears of grief with personal inadequacy and weakness. When bereaved children cry, adults often feel helpless. Out of a wish to protect the children (and themselves) from pain, well-meaning, misinformed adults often discourage crying through comments like, "You need to be strong for your mother," or "Tears won't bring him back," and, "He wouldn't want you to cry."

Another purpose of crying is postulated in the context of attachment theory, wherein tears are intended to bring about reunion with the person who has died. When a grieving six-year-old cries, he may be thinking (consciously or unconsciously) that his dead mother will return to comfort him. After all, she always hugged and kissed him when he cried before. The frequency and intensity of crying eventually wanes as the hoped-for reunion does not occur.

Tears are not a sign of weakness in children *or* adults. In fact, when bereaved children share tears they are indicating their willingness to do the work of mourning. As grief gardeners and other loving adults, we can better assist children by crying ourselves when we feel the need to.

Grief Misconception #9

Children are too young to understand death and religious beliefs about death.

Perhaps you have heard an adult say, "I'll just tell them he's gone to Heaven and that will take care of it." If only it were that simple! As one eight-year-old girl asked me, "If Grandpa is in Heaven, why did we put him in the ground?" Teaching abstract concepts about death and religion is no easy task, but it's one we must take seriously as we try to help bereaved children.

Grieving children need age-appropriate care. It is true that children are too young to **completely** understand death and the religious and spiritual belief systems surrounding death. Only over time will children assimilate these beliefs, and this developmental limitation must be respected. But no matter the specific beliefs of the family, the child must first be helped to understand that the person has died and cannot come back. It is a mistake to suggest that children need not mourn because the person who died "is in a better place anyway." To discourage children from mourning in this way is to set them up for a multitude of complications.

Many children naturally become frightened when they hear that after death people go to some poorly defined place (such as "the sky") for some poorly defined reason. For example, several times after a child has died I have learned that the surviving children—siblings and friends— had been told by their parents or church pastor that God needed a little boy or girl in heaven, so the child was "taken." I have counseled several children who were counting the days until they too would be "taken." Not surprisingly, these children were having trouble sleeping and were experiencing generalized feelings of anxiety. This kind of misguided communication can have long-term damaging effects on the child's emotional well-being.

In sum, caring adults need not feel guilty or ashamed if they cannot give specific definitions of God and Heaven, or what happens after death. Openness to mystery is valuable not only in teaching about death, but in teaching anything about life. On the other hand, neither should we proffer pseudo-explanations that may frighten or confuse children.

Grief Misconception #10
We should help children get over their grief.

Healthy mourning necessarily takes a long time—months, years and even lifetimes. In fact, children never overcome grief; they live with it and work to reconcile themselves to it.

As the bereaved child goes about his work of mourning, he begins to realize that life will be different without the person who died. Hope for a continued life emerges as the child is able to make commitments to the future, realizing the dead person will never be forgotten, yet knowing that his life can and will move forward.

No, children do not get over grief; they learn to live with it. Those who think the goal is to "resolve" grieving children's grief become destructive to the healing process.

✳ ✳ ✳

Being surrounded by adults who believe in these misconceptions invariably results in a heightened sense of isolation and alienation in bereaved children. A lack of support in the work of mourning destroys much of the grieving child's capacity to enjoy life, living, and loving. Bereaved children will experience the healing they deserve only when we, as individuals and as a society, are able to dispel these misconceptions.

Chapter Two

Mourning Styles: What Makes Each Child's Grief Unique?

No one, adult or child, grieves exactly as anyone else does, nor does one person grieve the deaths of different people in his or her life in the same way. Grief is never the same twice.

The companioning model I use when working with grieving children assumes that they know best about their own personal grief experiences. As caring adults and professional caregivers, our job is to observe their behaviors and listen to what they have to say—and to learn from them. Our job is never to prescribe what a bereaved child should be thinking or feeling. Instead, it is our job to listen and watch as she teaches us what her grief journey is like.

The factors that influence a child's grief are important things to listen and watch for. At times children themselves teach us about these influences, while at other times we can glean this information from significant adults in the grieving child's world. This chapter explores some of the main factors that influence the grief of children (though all influence the grief of adults, as well).

Of course, you will want to keep in mind that children do not enter my office announcing, "Today I would like to discuss some of the influences on my mourning." Nonetheless, it is my responsibility to patiently, compassionately, and gently encourage them to teach me about these influences.

I find it helpful to remember the grief gardening concept as I learn about these many influences over time. I use my rake, hoe, or sometimes even my shovel as we dig gently around the edges of the child's pain. The concept of gardening pulls me back from a more traditional model of assessment in which I might be tempted to ask too many direct questions of the child.

As you consider how you will learn about these important influences with each new child in your care, you may find it helpful to keep the following in mind:

- Too many informational questions tend to push the child away from teaching me. If I am patient, the child will trust me enough to naturally begin teaching me about these influences. I'm always telling myself, "I must join the child where he is before I can in any way move with him."

- Watch for doors that lead to understanding these influences. As the bereaved child learns to trust me, she will teach me both verbally and nonverbally about these influences (e.g. through emotion in the face, body posture, repetitive themes in play, etc.). Responding to these cues at a feeling level as opposed to an intellectual level often will lead us to mutually deeper levels of understanding.

- Avoid premature interpretations of why a child acts or feels a certain way. This is a trap the medical model of assessment may invite you into. ("But I have to assess so I can treat!") Premature interpretation is often an unconscious way for the counselor to control and therefore feel less anxious. Yet, the paradox is you must give up control to companion and be taught by the child.

Influences on a Child's Grief

Many factors influence the way a child grieves, including gender, age, the child's personality, the way someone dies, the relationship the child had with the person who died, and others.

Relationship with the person who died

Each child's response to a death depends largely upon the relationship he or she had with the person who died. For example, children will naturally grieve differently the deaths of a parent, a grandparent, or a sibling.

Perhaps more important than the familial tie, however, is the closeness the child felt to the person who died. The death of a nearby but emotionally distant uncle may mean much less to a child than the death of a cousin who lives states away but with whom the child communicated via Facebook or texting. Even within the same family, different siblings will respond differently to the death of a relative based on each child's attachment to the person who died.

Also keep in mind that children are sometimes very close to non-family members, such as a teacher or daycare provider. When I was young, I would stop by a neighbor lady's house after school. We had a ritual that became very dear to me: while she cleaned my glasses, I would tell her what happened at school that day. It didn't matter that we weren't related; she was still my good friend.

I was 11 when my neighbor died. Though I struggled with a multitude of thoughts and feelings about her death, no one thought to talk to me about it. Neither my parents nor other adults allowed me to teach them what her death meant to me. Because my neighbor and I weren't related, my grief became disenfranchised. I was a forgotten mourner.

Just as you shouldn't assume that kinship ties determine the magnitude of grief, you shouldn't assume that attachment doesn't exist even in ambivalent relationships. I have seen several children in my work who have had parents die of alcohol dependency-related causes. Consistently they have taught me that while they loved the person who died, they hated the disease that killed that person. They hated the way the alcohol-dependent person's behavior was influenced by the chemical abuse. They have also taught me that they didn't so much mourn the loss of a good relationship as they mourned the loss of a relationship they *wished* they could have had.

The nature of the death

The circumstances surrounding a death have a tremendous impact on a child's grief. As you help grieving kids do the work of mourning, be aware of the following four influences:

1. anticipated vs. sudden death

2. the age of the person who died

3. the child's sense of culpability for the death

4. the stigma surrounding the death

Anticipated vs. sudden death

Anticipating a death, such as one caused by prolonged illness, has the potential of assisting the child in adapting to the death. All too often, though, children are excluded from anticipatory grief by adults who want to protect them from pain.

Sudden, traumatic death and the grieving child

Unfortunately, today's children are exposed to violent deaths in many forms. They have been taught, through the media and through the realities of their own day-to-day lives, that people die senselessly. That people often kill other people. That people kill themselves. That people take drugs or alcohol and then drive, often killing others.

But when a child is personally impacted by sudden or accidental death, homicide, or suicide, she is not often taught about her unique grief and its healthy expression. You can help by understanding the special needs of survivors of sudden and traumatic death.

Sudden, traumatic deaths often leave survivors feeling numb and shocked for weeks and even months. Whether the death was natural (as in a heart attack) or accidental (as in a car crash), the bereaved child will probably have a hard time acknowledging the reality of the death. She will probably need extra support in the first weeks and months following the death.

- **Death by homicide** also creates overwhelming grief for survivors. Murder results in survivors grieving not only the death, but how the person died. A life has been cut short through an act of cruelty. The disregard for human life adds overwhelming feelings of turmoil, distrust, injustice, and helplessness to the child's normal sense of loss and sorrow.

  Survivors of murder victims enter into a world that is not understood by most people. A sad reality is that members of a community where a tragic murder has occurred sometimes blame the victim or survivors. Out of a need to protect themselves from their own personal feelings of vulnerability, some people reason that what has happened has to be somebody's fault. This need to "place blame" is projected in an effort to fight off any thoughts that such a tragedy would ever happen to them.

- **Death by suicide** is stigmatized in our society. In general we believe that suicide is wrong and talking about it makes us uncomfortable. If a child's father dies of a heart attack or is killed in a random shooting, he may receive lots of loving support from those around him. But if his father completes suicide, the child may be left to grieve in isolation.

A child's grief following a sudden, traumatic death is always complex. Don't be surprised by the intensity of her feelings. Accept that she may be struggling with a multitude of emotions more intense than those experienced after other types of death. Confusion, disorganization, fear, vulnerability, guilt, or anger are just a few of the emotions survivors may feel.

A child survivor of sudden or violent death may also feel intense anger. Her sense of injustice about the nature of the death can turn the normal anger of grief into rage. Remember—anger is not right or wrong, good or bad, appropriate or not appropriate. Do not try to diminish the anger, for it is in expressing rage that it begins to lose some of its power. Ultimately, healthy grief requires that these explosive emotions be expressed, not repressed.

Feelings of anxiety, panic, and fear are also normal. The child may feel threatened and unprotected. The world no longer feels as safe as it once did. Fear of what the future holds, fear that more sudden deaths might occur, an increased awareness of one's own mortality, feelings of vulnerability about being able to survive without the person, an inability to concentrate, and emotional and physical fatigue all serve to heighten anxiety, panic, and fear.

The unanswerable question, "But, why?" naturally comes up for survivors of a traumatic, violent death. The grieving child is searching to understand how something like this could happen. This doesn't mean you must answer the "why?" question. Bereaved children need a safe place to think, talk, and play out their feelings about this question more than they need a pat answer.

If, for example, Uncle Jeff has been dying of cancer for two years but his nine-year-old nephew Eric has been "protected" from this fact, Eric will be shocked when Uncle Jeff dies—and certainly less prepared than he would have been if the adults in his life had talked to him about the impending death at his level of understanding. To outsiders, then, what sometimes looks like an anticipated death is really a sudden death to an uninformed child.

Also keep in mind that children who are truly allowed to participate in anticipatory grief may still be in a lot of pain after the death. The fact that they were somewhat "prepared" for the death shouldn't minimize their need to mourn.

Sudden death, on the other hand, does not allow the child to emotionally prepare for grief's impact. The more sudden the death, the more likely the child is to mourn in doses and to push away some of the pain at first. Following an unexpected death, grieving children may even respond with an apparent lack of feelings. Don't be surprised, for example, if the little girl whose mother just died responds to the news by going outside to play on the swing set. She is protecting herself from this painful reality in the only way she knows how. You may see even *less* outward mourning in the child who experiences a sudden death than in the child who experiences an anticipated death.

Age of the person who died

The age of the person who died can impact the child's psychological and spiritual integration of the death. The natural order of the world says that older people die first: grandparents, then parents, then their children (when they have become grandparents themselves.) Like many of us, children often believe that only old people die, or that only old people *should* die. The older a person is, the more acceptable the death.

For a child, the death of a parent seems "out of order." Not only does the child lose a primary caregiver, but he also loses the chance to spend time with the parent later in life and to enjoy the prospect of having grandparents around for his own children. Moreover, the child whose parent has died can feel a sense of awkwardness or anger because most other children his age still have parents. This grief-borne form of "peer pressure" only underscores the child's sense that his parent died "too young." (For more on the death of a parent, see the end of this chapter.)

Of course, if a parent is too young to die, another child is much too young to die. What's more, when a child's sibling or friend dies, another young person has died; confronting this reality can mean confronting the possibility of one's own death—a very scary prospect for children.

The child's sense of culpability for the death

Due to the developmental concept of "magical thinking," in which children sometimes believe that thoughts cause action, the bereaved child might feel a sense of responsibility for a death. What child, for example, hasn't wished that her sibling would just go away and leave her alone forever? If this sibling dies, then, the grieving child may well feel guilty. Giving children accurate information about why and how a death occurred can help ease their consciences and allow them to move forward in their grief journeys.

On the other hand, in our increasingly violent society, children sometimes actually are responsible for the death of someone else, intentionally or not. Almost every day in our metropolitan newspapers we read about the accidental shooting death of a child at the hands of another child, for example. In these cases, the bereaved child will most certainly feel overwhelming guilt. I recommend that these children receive professional guidance in exploring their culpability and how it will change their lives.

The potential stigma surrounding the death

Sometimes there is a stigma surrounding the nature of the death. The greater the stigma, generally the less the support available to the child and family as they mourn. Examples of stigmatized deaths include those from AIDS, suicide, homicide, and drug overdose. My colleague Ken Doka has described losses that cannot be openly acknowledged, socially sanctioned, or publicly mourned as "disenfranchised grief" experiences. The potential of stigma should always be kept in mind as you companion grieving children and their families.

The child's unique personality

Each child has a unique personality that affects the ways in which he or she mourns. Some kids are talkative while others are quiet. Some are boisterous while others are reserved. These personality styles, which existed long before the death, will influence the child's mourning style.

For example, the naturally retiring child may be accustomed to working through stresses on her own. For her, temporarily withdrawing from others may help her do her work of mourning. Another child may tend to wear his feelings on his sleeve. This child may let everyone know that he is in pain after someone he loves dies.

As kids move toward adolescence, their personalities may seem to change somewhat, and it may be harder to distinguish between behaviors brought about by developmental stresses and behaviors associated with grief. My experience suggests that it doesn't really matter which is which. All behaviors are multiply determined anyway, and trying to separate their causes is beside the point.

The important thing to note here is that there is no right way to mourn. All mourning styles are OK, provided that the child hasn't changed dramatically due to the death. If, for instance, a formerly gregarious child withdraws completely from friends and family, this is a sign that she needs extra bereavement help. The opposite is also true. If a formerly withdrawn child starts getting in fights, that's a symptom of an underlying grief need that's not being met. In adolescents, look for red flag behaviors such as suicidal actions, sexual acting out, and eating disorders.

Unique characteristics of the person who died

Just as the personality of the bereaved child is reflected in his or her expression of grief, so too are the unique characteristics of the person who died. While some people have personalities that allow children to be close to them, others can make it difficult for children to connect.

Another aspect of personality is the role the person who died played within the family system. If, for example, the family patriarch dies— perhaps the grandfather—the child may feel a compounded sense of loss when the family no longer gathers at grandpa's house. Not only has the child lost a grandfather, but perhaps contact with her aunts, uncles, and cousins, as well.

The child's age

A number of researchers have studied the ways in which chronological age affects the child's response to loss. In general, these studies found that children five and under tend not to fully understand death, particularly death's finality. For children older than five, the studies had divergent findings. One found that children six and older may understand that death is final, while another found that only children nine years and older have realistic perceptions of death.

That difference in meaning is a product of each child's life experiences to date. Those who at a young age have already had several people they love die are more likely to fully understand death, for example. On the other hand, children who have never experienced the death of someone loved or, just as important, haven't been lovingly taught by adults about death, are more likely to harbor inaccurate notions of the concept. Moreover, other factors such as self-concept and intelligence also have an important role in the individual child's understanding of death.

Social expectations based on the child's gender

This influence on grief stems from the different ways in which boys and girls are taught to express their feelings. Generally, boys are encouraged to be strong and exercise restraint in expressing painful feelings. Because of this, boys often have more difficulty in allowing themselves to feel helpless and express their grief.

Girls, too, may encounter socially-engendered difficulties in expressing their grief. While they may have been taught to show sadness, they are often also taught that for them, anger is bad — especially physical expression of that anger. So, sometimes in little girls, appropriate grief-borne anger gets repressed.

We as caregivers must stay sensitive to this gender conditioning. Unfortunately, we can't control how children have already been conditioned, but we can help them express those feelings they sometimes feel ashamed to have. For example, you might encourage both boys and girls to physically release pent-up emotions by participating in sports.

Cultural/ethnic background

The grieving child's response to death is impacted by his or her cultural and ethnic backgrounds. Different cultures are known for the various ways they express or repress their grief. As caregivers we must remember to be careful about defining "normal" responses of both bereaved children and adults. Normal mourning (means of expression, length considerations, etc.) varies widely from culture to culture.

Keening, for example, is a process of lamenting for the dead. It is usually expressed in a very loud, wailing voice or sometimes in

Helping infants and toddlers when someone they love dies

Due to their age, infants and toddlers demand special mention. Many adults think that because very young children are not completely aware of what is going on around them, they are not impacted by death. We must dispel this misconception. I say it simply: Any child old enough to love is old enough to mourn.

True, infants and toddlers are not developmentally mature enough to fully understand the concept of death. In fact, many children do not truly understand the inevitability and permanence of death until adolescence.

But understanding death and being affected by it are two very different things. When a primary caregiver dies, even tiny babies notice and react to the loss. They might not know exactly what happened and why, but they do know that someone important is now missing from their small worlds.

This section contains practical tips for primary caregivers to grieving infants and toddlers. If you are counseling a parent or other caregiver to a bereaved infant or toddler, you may want to photocopy this section for their use.

The special needs of grieving infants

As anyone who has been around infants knows, babies quickly bond with their mothers or other primary caregivers. In fact, studies have shown that babies just hours old recognize and respond to their mothers' voices. Many psychologists even believe that babies think they and their mothers are one and the same person for a number of months.

This powerful and exclusive attachment to mommy and daddy continues through most of the first year of life. When a parent dies, then, there is no question the baby notices that something is missing. She will likely protest her loss by crying more than usual, sleeping more or less than she did before, or changing her eating patterns.

- **Offer comfort**
  When they are upset, most infants are soothed by physical contact. Pick up the bereaved infant when he cries. Wear him in a front pack; he will be calmed by your heartbeat and motion. Give him a gentle baby massage. Talk to him and smile at him as much as possible.

And do not worry about spoiling him. The more you hold him, rock him and sing to him, the more readily he will realize that though things have changed, someone will always be there to take care of him.

- **Take care of basic needs**
  Besides lots of love, an infant needs to be fed, sheltered, diapered, and bathed. Try to maintain the grieving baby's former schedule. But don't be surprised if she sleeps or eats more or less than usual. Such changes are her way of showing her grief. If she starts waking up several times a night, soothe her back to sleep.

  The most important thing you can do is to meet her needs—whatever they seem to be—quickly and lovingly in the weeks and months to come.

The special needs of grieving toddlers

Like infants, bereaved toddlers mostly need our love and attention. They also need us to help them understand that though it is painful, grief is the price we pay for the priceless chance to love others. They need us to teach them that death is a normal and natural part of life.

- **Offer comfort and care.**
  The bereaved toddler needs one-on-one care 24 hours a day. Make sure someone she loves and trusts is always there to feed her, clothe her, diaper her, and play with her. Unless she is already comfortable with a certain provider, now is not the time to put her in daycare.

  Expect regressive behaviors from grieving toddlers. Those who slept well before may now wake up during the night. Independent children may now be afraid to leave their parents' side. Formerly potty-trained kids may need diapers again. All of these behaviors are normal grief responses. They are the toddler's way of saying, "I'm upset by this death and I need to be taken care of right now." By tending to her baby-like needs, you will be letting her know that she *will* be taken care of and that she is loved without condition.

- **Model your own grief.**
  Toddlers learn by imitation. If you grieve in healthy ways, toddlers will learn to do the same. Don't hide your feelings when you're around children. Instead, share them. Cry if you want to. Be angry if you want to. Let the toddler know that these painful feelings are not directed at him and are not his fault, however.

  Sometimes you may feel so overwhelmed by your own grief that you can't make yourself emotionally available to the bereaved toddler.

You needn't feel guilty about this; it's OK to need some "alone time" to mourn. In fact, the more fully you allow yourself to do your own work of mourning, the sooner you'll be available to help the child. In the meantime, make sure other caring adults are around to nurture the grieving toddler.

- **Use simple, concrete language.**
  When someone a toddler loves dies, he will know that person is missing. He may ask for Mommy or Uncle Ted one hundred times a day. I recommend using the word "dead" in response to his queries. Say, "Mommy is dead, honey. She can never come back." Though he won't yet know what "dead" means, he will begin to differentiate it from "bye-bye" or "gone" or "sleeping"—terms that only confuse the issue. Tell him that dead means the body stops working. The person can't walk or talk anymore, can't breathe, and can't eat. And while using simple, concrete language is important, remember that more than two-thirds of your support will be conveyed nonverbally.

- **Keep change to a minimum.**
  All toddlers need structure, but bereaved toddlers, especially, need their daily routines. Keeping mealtimes, bedtime, and bath time the same lets them know that their life continues and that they will always be cared for. And try not to implement other changes right away. Now is not the time to go from a crib to a bed, to potty train, or to wean from a bottle.

Helping Infants and Toddlers After Someone They Love Dies Brochure
This information is also available in a brochure as a part of The Helping Series, a set of brochures for easy distribution to clients and families. Visit www.centerforloss.com and click on Brochures to order.

a wordless crying out. Some cultures encourage and legitimize keening while others don't understand it and sometimes perceive it as "pathological." Ireland, Crete, China, and Mexico are among those countries where you are more likely to see the bereaved keening.

Cultures that encourage outward expressions of grief such as keening are more likely to instill healthy mourning practices in the grieving child. Mourning-avoiding cultures, on the other hand, like those prevalent in American Anglo society today, often make a child's grief journey more difficult. As we know, the repression of grief can have negative repercussions long into the bereaved child's adulthood. We can find another example in Latino cultures. For Latin Americans, it is important to "take care of your own"—which means the grieving child may not be able to seek outside help. Emotional outlets such as bereavement support groups may not be seen as "necessary."

Religious/spiritual influences

Religious and spiritual backgrounds, which are of course very closely tied to cultural and ethnic backgrounds, also influence the child's grief response. I truly believe that to be a growth-oriented companion to bereaved children, I must be sensitive not only to the psychological dimensions of the child's world, but to the religious and spiritual dimensions as well. Children by their very nature are spiritual beings! If we ignore this, we don't allow them to teach us about this vital part of themselves.

Many of us trained in traditional mental health settings were literally taught to ignore religious and spiritual issues in the lives of those we work with as counselors. Some of us may have even been taught that "religious or spiritual problems" are merely symptoms of deeper psychological problems. But in my growing experience, I find there to be a spiritual dimension to every life crisis, particularly death. If we allow it, death penetrates the defensive shell of (assumed) invulnerability that most North Americans wear. Fortunately, most children have not yet donned this defensive armor and openly enter into teaching us adults about religious and spiritual experiences.

We must ask ourselves what belief systems undergird and give meaning to the life of this child and family. Even though these beliefs may be different than my own, how can I understand and acknowledge them in the life of this child? If the child tells me (as many have) that her mom or dad, grandma or grandpa, brother or sister, is "watching over them," how do I understand this?

Grief: ages and stages

I am not a believer in the theory that children of a certain age grieve in a certain way. Each child's responses—cognitive, social, emotional, spiritual, and physical—to the death of someone loved are different.

Still, it is true that a child's developmental level affects her mourning. The chart that follows tries to capture some of the most common grief responses of children in different age categories. But remember—an individual child should not be stuffed into a textbook category. As companions, we must let each bereaved child teach us what grief is like for him.

	Typical grief responses	Companioning tips
Infants and toddlers (Baby - age two) *Loss may be understood as an absence, particularly of a primary caregiver.*	"I'm upset" behaviors (e.g. crying more, thumb sucking, biting.)	Offer physical comfort.
	Changes in normal patterns. May sleep more or less, eat more or less, be fussier.	Accept the changes while still trying to adhere to some kind of routine. Infants and toddlers are typically comforted by the structure of routines.
Preschoolers (Ages 3-6) *Death may be thought of as temporary and/ or reversible.*	May not understand their new, scary feelings and may not be able to verbalize what is happening inside them.	Provide them with terms for some of their feelings: grief, sadness, numb.
	May ask questions about the death over and over again. During play may reenact the death.	Answer concretely and lovingly. Be honest. Don't tell half-truths. "Death" play is fine and helps children integrate the reality of the death. You may want to join in and offer your guidance.
	May regress: cling to parents, suck thumb, lose potty training, baby talk, etc.	Short-term regressive behaviors are normal. Offer your presence and support.

	Typical grief responses	Companioning tips
Grade schoolers (Ages 6-11) *A clearer understanding of death develops. Older kids in this age group may have an "adult" understanding of what death is.*	Children in this age group continue to express their grief primarily through play. May "hang back" socially and scholastically.	Use "older kid" play therapy techniques, especially for 10-12 year-olds. Children need permission to concentrate on mourning before they can be expected to forge ahead with the rest of their lives. Give them time.
	May act out because they don't know how else to handle their grief feelings.	Offer constructive "venting" alternatives. Support groups can be very helpful.
Adolescents (Ages 12 and up) *Understand death cognitively but are only beginning to grapple with it spiritually.*	May protest the loss by acting out and/or withdrawing.	Acting out behaviors should be tolerated if the teen or others is not being harmed. Withdrawal is normal in the short-term. (Long-term withdrawal is a sign the teen needs extra help.)
	May feel life has been unfair to them, act angry.	A teen's normal egocentrism can cause him to focus exclusively on the effect the death has had on him and his future. After he has had time to explore this issue, encourage him to consider the death's impact on the larger social group: family, friends, etc.
	May act out a search for meaning. May test his own mortality.	Teens begin to really explore the "why" questions about life and death. Encourage this search for meaning unless it may harm the teen or others.

Do the belief systems I learn about from the child and family help or hinder the healing process? In other words, is their religion or spirituality crippling or creative?

In some belief systems, for example, mourning implies that you are not a true believer. After all, their doctrines reason, the dead person has gone to Heaven—the most wonderful place imaginable. Why be sad at this miraculous passage? Because, the grieving child may say to himself, I *am* sad. I do feel bad/angry/guilty etc. Religious systems that deny a child the healthy expression of these normal grief responses only cause the child to feel confused and emotionally and spiritually stifled.

On the other hand, many families recognize that having faith and mourning are not mutually exclusive. They allow and encourage children to be open to the mysteries of both life and death. A personal goal for me is to nurture in people of all ages a high level of spiritual wellness. (This often is much easier accomplished with children than adults.) Companioning grieving kids demands that we as caregivers be holistic, seeking to enable healing and growth in all dimensions— psychological as well as spiritual and religious.

I should note that I sometimes must gently confront religious or spiritual messages from adults to children that I believe might complicate the child's healing journey (e.g. "We have faith, so we don't need to be sad.") This kind of message is growth-blocking, not growth-enhancing. With gentle respect and timely pacing, I attempt to help re-frame for these families the need to mourn despite having faith. It doesn't always work, but I feel an ethical and spiritual obligation to try.

Other crises/stresses in the child's life

Death and loss seldom occur in isolation. To understand the impact of a death on a child, you must also understand other losses the child is experiencing concurrently. Sometimes two or more people a child loves will die around the same time. This, of course, may overwhelm the child and may complicate his mourning.

On the other hand, sometimes additional stresses on the child at the time of the death are good stresses. Say, for example, a child's grandfather dies about the same time her mother gives birth to a new baby. In this case the birth of the baby may actually delay the child's mourning because the child (like most of us) will choose to focus on the happy event first.

Secondary losses

When someone we love dies, we don't just lose the presence of that person. As a result of the death, we may lose many other connections to ourselves and our world. Children feel these secondary losses, too.

Secondary losses include the loss of friends and community due to a geographical move, loss of security if the breadwinner in the family has died, and loss of childhood if the child has been forced to "grow up" prematurely because of the death. In short, the death of someone loved will often cause a ripple effect of other losses.

As you companion the bereaved child, keep in mind the following common secondary losses that can make the grief experience more complex.

Loss of self

- self ("Part of me died, too, when my Mommy died.")
- identity (The child may have to rethink her role as child or sibling.)
- self-confidence (Child mourners often feel shame or a lessened sense of self-esteem.)
- health (Physical symptoms of mourning.)
- personality ("I'm just not myself . . .")

Loss of security

- emotional security (Parent/caretaker is now gone, causing emotional upheaval.)
- physical security (A grieving child may worry who will take care of her physical needs.)
- fiscal security (A bereaved child may be concerned about family finances.)
- lifestyle (Child may be used to a boisterous and loving family life, but that life is now quieted due to the death of a family member.)

Loss of meaning

- goals & dreams (Dreams for future can be shattered, goals can seem unreachable without person who died.)
- faith (Mourners often question faith.)
- will/desire to live ("Why go on?")
- joy (Life's most meaningful emotion—happiness—is compromised by the death of someone loved.)

Prior experiences with death

A grieving child's past experiences with death greatly affect the ways in which he or she will respond to the most recent loss. Children who have been taught, for example, to repress their grief will typically fall back on that impulse whenever someone loved dies. The more negative the prior experiences with death, the more complicated each new encounter.

The **number** of losses children have experienced also affects their grief responses. Some children grow up in environments that expose them to losses from the time they're born. Children who live in foster home after foster home, for example, confront loss every time they must leave a family. Inexplicably, other children encounter an inordinate number of losses early on. One eight-year-old boy I counseled, for instance, had already experienced the unrelated deaths of seven people he loved.

Bereavement overload such as this can cause **attachment disorders.** Consciously or unconsciously, these children reason that bonding with others does no good and, in fact, can cause great pain. "If I don't love anyone," they think, "I won't get hurt again." In general, children with extensive loss histories are more prone to both attachment disorders and acting-out behavior.

On the other end of the spectrum are children who **never** encounter death in their young lives. As I mentioned earlier, ours is the first "death-free" generation. It isn't unusual for today's children to reach early- or mid-adulthood before someone close to them dies. As a result, some don't learn that death and loss are an integral part of life.

The child who hasn't been exposed to death may not know what to do with his grief when someone loved does die. In such cases, especially, it is important for adults to model healthy mourning because inexperienced grievers learn through imitation.

The child's ritual/funeral experiences

Most of the rituals in our society focus on children. What would birthdays or Christmas be without kids? Unfortunately, the funeral ritual, whose purpose is to help grieving people begin to heal, is not seen as a ritual for children. Too often, children are not included in the funeral because adults want to protect them. The funeral is painful, they reason, so I will shelter the children from this pain.

Yes, funerals can be very painful, but children have the same right and privilege to participate in them as adults do. Funerals are important to survivors because they:

- help survivors acknowledge that someone has died.

- provide a structure to support and assist them through their initial period of mourning.

- provide a time to honor, remember, and affirm the life of the person who died.

- allow for a "search for meaning" within the context of each person's religious or philosophical values.

Thus, if a bereaved child has not been included in the funeral ritual, he or she may have a more difficult time acknowledging that someone loved has died and embarking on the grief journey. Moreover, if the child was allowed to attend the funeral but wasn't gently guided through the experience by caring adults, he or she may have questions or even fears about what happened. Asking grieving children age-appropriate questions about their funeral experiences will help you better understand how this ritual has affected their grief journeys.

Additional Influences

Finally, it's important to consider a child's physical condition and school and peer situations when you are serving as grief companion.

Physical health influences

A holistic understanding of the child requires awareness of the child's physical condition. An excellent standard of care is to have any child you work with in counseling get a good general medical examination. Why? Just like adults, children's bodies respond to the stress of the death of someone loved. Actually, school nurses, pediatricians, and family physicians are among those who most commonly refer children to me for help.

In many situations, the physical "hurts" the child expresses are a form of emotional communication. After all, we often teach children that when you don't feel well (whether emotionally, spiritually or physically), the most immediate way to receive attention is to be "sick." Even very young children pick up on these cues. If the child is in a closed family system where open mourning is discouraged, this tendency is heightened. The child unconsciously reasons, "If I can't play it out, act it out, or talk it out, I'll get sick—and then maybe I'll get nurtured." Aren't kids smart!

Learning disabilities, injury, illness, and hospitalization are obviously loss experiences for children. To experience bereavement on top of these types of losses may create normal feelings of physical vulnerability and, in general, unwellness. A child with concerns about his own physical well-being ("Will I die too?") will often express these concerns indirectly through a preoccupation with his health.

School Influences

Children spend much of their time in school. Consulting with school personnel about observations of a child, before and after a death in the child's life, can provide you with valuable information as you work to better understand the life of the child. Teachers are often very open to working collaboratively with counselors in efforts to help children impacted by grief.

Moreover, a compassionate teacher, school counselor, or principal may be one of the bereaved child's major supporters. We can help them know how to compassionately be present to the child. We can also sensitize school personnel to the importance of recognizing that grief is a process, not an event. Loss histories in the life of the child should be passed along as the child progresses through school.

When I was first getting started with my work in this area, one of my favorite things to do was go around to schools and invite myself to provide them with in-service trainings. While I was rejected by some (I shouldn't have expected any less in this mourning-avoiding culture), many schools received me with enthusiasm.

Peer Influences

Perhaps the most instinctive place children turn when in crisis is to their peers. The companioning approach mandates us to work to determine who the grieving child's friends are. After all, peers are often the ones who let us adults know when one of their friends is struggling in some way.

Children appear to have an almost intuitive sense of the emotional and spiritual well-being of their friends. Any concerns they express about a peer should be taken seriously.

Many bereaved children feel different than their peers who haven't been impacted by death. Some kids will move toward other children who have had similar losses, seeking support and understanding. Interestingly, other kids will try to ignore their new "difference" (being bereaved) and project a need to be just the same as everyone else. The problem is that everything *isn't* the same. They may project feeling ashamed that they are no longer a "family," for example.

As caregivers we can encourage supportive peer contact and play activities as the child doses herself in her grief journey. In the midst of change, the constant of peers is critically important in the life of the grieving child.

A Deeper Look: Death Within the Family

For children, death of immediate family members is always more difficult. Let's take a deeper look at key relationships and grieving.

When a parent dies

The death of a parent is, without a doubt, one of the most painful experiences in a child's life. It leaves a permanent imprint on the child. Even when reconciliation unfolds, this profound loss will never be forgotten.

Perhaps the most important influence on the child's grief journey will be the response of the surviving parent or other important adults in the child's life. Obviously, the surviving parent will be less available to the child than she was prior to the death. We don't want to shame her for this but instead encourage her to seek support for her own work of mourning. As her mourning progresses she will become more available to the child. If, on the other hand, the surviving parent (or other significant caregiving adult) continues to be immobilized by her own grief, the bereaved child may suffer not only from the death, but from the feeling of being isolated emotionally from the surviving parent.

The death of a parent also frequently results in numerous accompanying losses for the child, such as changed financial status, moves requiring changes in friends, schools, etc. At a time when the child's world has been turned upside down by the death of a parent, these additional losses may overwhelm the child and put him at risk for retreating from life.

Another important lesson many grieving kids have taught me after the death of a parent is that they wonder if they are still a family without a mom or dad. The child needs help in redefining himself as he searches to find meaning in going on without the dead parent. Maintaining faith in his future may be a real struggle. The child may in effect ask himself, "What meaning will my life have without this important person?"

Sometimes children act out their wish to be reunited with a dead parent through fantasizing their own deaths. Some "death play" is

Helping children with funerals

When children have the opportunity to participate in a funeral, they have a better chance of integrating their loss. Unless they have attended one before, children don't know what to expect from a funeral. You and the child's parents can help by explaining what will happen before, during, and after the ceremony. Let the child's questions and natural curiosity guide the discussion.

Give as many specifics as the child seems interested in hearing. You might tell her how the room will look, who will be coming, and how long everyone will be there, for example. When possible, arrange for the child to visit the funeral home before the funeral.

If the body will be viewed either at a visitation or at the funeral itself, let the child know this in advance. Explain what the casket and the body will look like. If the body is to be cremated, explain what cremation means and what will happen to the ashes. Be sure the child understands that because the person is dead, he doesn't feel pain or anything at all during cremation.

Also help children anticipate that they will see people expressing a wide variety of emotions at the funeral. They will see tears, straight faces, and laughter. If adults are able to openly show feelings, including crying, children will feel much more free to express a sense of loss at their own level.

- *Help children understand the why of funerals*—Children need to know that the funeral is a time of sadness because someone has died, a time to honor the person who died, a time to help comfort and support each other, and a time to affirm that life goes on.

  One why children seem to embrace easily is that funerals are a time to say goodbye. And saying goodbye helps us all acknowledge that the person we loved is gone and cannot come back. If the body is to be viewed, tell the child that seeing the body helps people say goodbye and that he may touch the person he loved once last time.

  Now is also a good time to explain to the child what spiritual significance the funeral has for you and your family. This can be difficult, for even adults have a hard time articulating their beliefs about life and death. One guideline: children have difficulty understanding abstractions, so it is best to use concrete terms when talking about religious concepts.

- **Include children in the ritual**—When appropriate, you might invite children not only to attend the funeral but to take part in it. Grieving children feel like their feelings "matter" when they can share a favorite memory or read a special poem as part of the funeral. Shyer children can participate by lighting a candle or placing something special (a memento or a photo, for example) in the casket. And many children feel more included when they are invited to help plan the funeral service.

  Children should be encouraged to attend and participate in funerals, but never forced. When they are lovingly guided through the process, however, most children **want** to attend. Offer the reticent child options: "You can come to the visitation today with everyone else or if you want, I can take just you this morning so you can say goodbye in private."

- **Understand and accept the child's way of mourning**—Do not prescribe to children what they should feel or for how long—particularly during the funeral. Remember that children often need to accept their grief in doses, and that outward signs of grief may come and go. It is not unusual, for example, for children to want to roughhouse with their cousins during the visitation or play video games right after the funeral. Instead of punishing this behavior, you should respect the child's need to be a child during this extraordinarily difficult time. If the child's behavior is disturbing others, explain that there are acceptable and unacceptable ways to act at funerals and that you expect the child to consider the feelings of other mourners—including yours.

Helping Children with Funerals Brochure
This information is also available in a brochure as a part of The Helping Series, a set of brochures for easy distribution to clients and families. Visit www.centerforloss.com and click on Brochures to order.

normal, but adult caregivers must be careful not to make heaven seem so attractive that the child would prefer to die and be with her dead parent.

Helping a child who has a parent die is the epitome of good preventive mental and spiritual health care. The potential long-term effects of not being companioned well at this time are many, including difficulties with future intimate relationships, vocational success, and general joy of life.

When a sibling dies

Next to the death of a parent, the death of a sibling can be the most traumatic event in a child's life. Why? Because not only has a family member died, but a family member for whom the child probably had very strong and ambivalent feelings. As those of us who have brothers and sisters know, sibling relationships are characterized by anger, jealousy, and a fierce closeness and love—a highly complex mixture of emotion. This complexity colors the surviving child's grief experience.

I have had the privilege of companioning hundreds of bereaved siblings. Among many other special lessons, they have taught me they often feel:

- *Guilt.* For a number of reasons, grieving siblings often feel guilty. Their power of "magical thinking"—believing that thoughts cause actions—might make them think they literally caused the death. "Sam died because I sometimes wished he would go away forever" is a common response among children who haven't been given the concrete details of the sibling's death and who haven't been assured that they were not at fault.

- *Relief.* A child may also feel relief as well as pain when a sibling dies. Responses such as, "Now no one will take my things" or "I'm glad I have a room to myself" are natural and do not mean the child didn't love his sibling. It is important that you provide an atmosphere in which the child feels safe to express whatever he may be feeling.

- *Fear.* When a child's brother or sister dies, another young person has died. So, for a child, confronting this reality can mean confronting the possibility of one's own death. Be prepared to honestly but reassuringly answer questions such as, "Will I die, too?" The death of a sibling can also make a bereaved child fear that one or all of her other family members will die, too, leaving her alone.

- *Confusion.* One eight-year-old girl I counseled after the death of her brother asked me, "Am I still a big sister?" This little girl was obviously struggling with the confusing task of redefining herself, both within the family unit and the world at large. The answer to her question, of course, is both yes and no, but ultimately it is a question the child must answer herself. Adults can help, however, by letting the child teach them what this confusion is like.

When a grandparent dies

When a grandparent dies, the grandchildren may or may not actively mourn.

Some children are extremely close to their grandparents; they may see them frequently and even overnight with them. In some cases grandparents even assume a primary parenting role for their grandchildren. When a grandparent to whom a child is close dies, the child can be profoundly affected. On the other hand, in our highly mobile culture some grandchildren rarely, if ever, see their grandparents. Naturally, these children may not express a need to mourn when a long-distance grandparents dies.

Still, don't assume that distance in child-grandparent relationships determines the depth of feelings. A child who lives down the street from his grandmother may feel less close to her than a child whose far-away grandmother writes, calls, or visits often.

We also know that many children feel disenfranchised after the death of a grandparent if the death is not openly acknowledged, publicly mourned, or socially supported. You may have heard people say, "Well, it was only his grandparent. The child has to have known that the grandparent would die someday." Obviously, these kinds of comments don't allow for the "teach me" philosophy emphasized throughout this book.

In families where grandparents were strong matriarchs or patriarchs, there is often a ripple-effect across generations as the family unit struggles to redefine itself. Perhaps the family doesn't get together as often as it did before grandma's death. Now the children may not see their cousins and aunts and uncles as often as they did before.

The personality of the grandparent also influences children's responses. Some older adults are naturals with children and the kids feel very close to them. Other older adults may have a difficult time relating to young children. Therefore, they may be around the children but still not create any kind of emotional bond. Think about your own grandparents. Did you find yourself relating differently and feeling closer to one grandparent over another?

As always, the key in companioning children through grief after the death of a grandparent is to let the children teach you about what the death means to them. Then, support them non-judgmentally in their need or lack of need to mourn the death.

When a child's pet dies

This topic may seem like it doesn't fit here, but children, especially young children, often perceive the family pet as an equal. The death of a pet is often a child's first introduction to death. Some of my happiest childhood memories were of time spent with my dog, Chico. But one day she ran out the door and was hit by a car. I'm not alone when I say that Chico was a member of my family. She slept with me, she played with me; she was not only my dog, but my loving friend.

No, our pets are not "just a dog" or "just a cat." With the death of a pet children experience a significant loss. As caring adults, we have the opportunity and responsibility to respond in ways that empower children to grieve for their pets. Your response during this time can help children's experiences be a positive or negative part of their personal growth and development.

- Model your own feelings about the death of the pet.
- When appropriate, explain that the pet's illness and death was no one's fault.
- Use simple and direct language in sharing facts about the death.
- If euthanasia is used, do not describe it as "putting the pet to sleep."
- Encourage involvement in ritual.
- Encourage creative outlets for feelings.
- Openly discuss what will be done with the pet's body.
- Do not attempt to replace the dead pet before the child has an opportunity to mourn.

※ ※ ※

Every child's grief is unique. How a child grieves and mourns is influenced by the relationship, circumstances, and child's age and environment when the death occurs. These factors, along with personality and temperament, also affect how a child will express grief emotionally. The next chapter takes a look at the unique ways children communicate their grief.

Chapter Three

Sad/Scared/Mad/Tired/Glad: How a Grieving Child Acts, Thinks, and Feels

It is easy to tell when flowers in the garden are under stress of some kind. Their leaves turn yellow, they droop, they fail to flower—all visible symptoms that let the gardener know something is wrong. Children, too, often express their underlying needs in ways we can see, typically through behaviors.

Grieving children can and often do undergo major emotional, spiritual, physical, and behavioral changes. As grief gardeners we can learn to understand these changes as symptomatic of underlying grief needs. This understanding will in turn help us to help the bereaved child.

This chapter presents some of the most typical feelings and thoughts grieving children experience—and the behavioral ways in which they express those feelings. Following a discussion of each grief dimension, I have included caregiving suggestions—things you can do to encourage the expression of each feeling.

✳ ✳ ✳ ✳ ✳ ✳ ✳ ✳ ✳ ✳

Twelve Dimensions of a Child's Grief

Children may express all or some of these responses to grief, in no particular order.

1. Shock/Apparent Lack of Feelings
2. Physiological Changes
3. Regression
4. Disorganization and Panic
5. Explosive Emotions
6. Acting-Out
7. Hyper-maturity
8. Fear
9. Guilt
10. Relief
11. Sadness
12. Reconciliation

✳ ✳ ✳ ✳ ✳ ✳ ✳ ✳ ✳ ✳

"Daddy is *not* dead. I'm going to go play now!"

Dimension 1. Shock/Apparent Lack of Feelings

As you might expect, children often initially feel a sense of emotional shock when someone they love dies. The child may say or think, "No, this didn't happen. Daddy's not dead. He'll come back," or, "If I pretend this isn't happening, then maybe it won't be." The mind blocks and at times is not connected to what the child hears. Actually, "shock" is a generic term that subsumes a variety of emotions, such as disbelief, numbness, and denial, as well as physiological responses.

Sometimes outside observers jump to the conclusion that the child's disbelief or apparent lack of feelings means a complete denial of, or even indifference to, the death. Parents often have difficulty understanding, for example, how Josh can be out in the backyard playing only an hour after learning of Grandpa's death. They frequently feel hurt and angry with a child's apparent lack of feelings, and as a result, sometimes end up distancing themselves from the child.

In fact, the bereaved child's apparent lack of feelings serves a very useful purpose. Often children "dose" their early grief by allowing just a little reality in at a time. In this way they move toward their grief—at their own pace—instead of away from it. When the full reality of the death seeps through, children may well do some "catch-up grieving" as previously blocked thoughts and feelings surface.

Pay attention to the ways in which other adults respond to the child's apparent lack of feelings. Many will tacitly affirm this stoicism because our society advocates facing trauma without showing feeling. The person who doesn't cry when someone dies is most often the one whom others believe "took things so well." So, while the child receives this destructively affirmative message from some adults, others simply can't understand why the child is not grieving and ask themselves if the child really loved the person who died. The result is that the child is frequently stuck in the middle not knowing what to think, feel, or do.

While it is critical to allow grieving children this initial period of numbness, we must be careful never to inappropriately encourage a child to suppress other emotional responses. It is cruel to reinforce a child's belief that Dad will come home, for example, when we realize this is impossible. At times, adults' difficulty in explaining the finality of death to children makes them confused about what to think or feel. And admonishments like, "Be strong," "You shouldn't cry," and "Well, now you will have to carry on," often encourage the suppression of emotions and as a result reinforce a prolonged sense of denial.

This experience of shock, denial, numbness and apparent lack of feelings is typically most intense during the first several months after the death. However, to see this dimension of the child's grief recur suddenly is not at all uncommon, particularly on the anniversary of the death or on other special occasions (birthday, Christmas, etc.). I also have witnessed this dimension when the child visits a place associated with a special memory of the dead person.

The companion's helping role with shock

- *Accept the child's apparent lack of feelings as a natural response.* The major role of the grief gardener during this period of shock is to keep the grieving child in touch with a supportive, caring part of her world. You can also educate the child's parents or other caretakers about the naturalness of this response.

- *Talk "with," not "at," the child about the death.* The tendency to talk "at" instead of "with" a bereaved child is often a reflection of our frustration that the child isn't responding. It's OK to spend time just being with the child who isn't yet ready to embrace his pain; don't feel you need to make a counseling breakthrough at the first session.

- *Respect the child's need to talk, or not to talk, about the death.* Grief gardeners respect a child's need to move in and out of grief. Most grieving children will provide cues when they feel comfortable and safe talking about the person who has died. Moreover, a child will often test adults to see if they feel comfortable communicating their own thoughts and feelings about the loss. As you build a relationship with the child based on sensitivity, warmth, and understanding, the child will feel more comfortable sharing her grief with you.

"My stomach hurts!"
Dimension 2. Physiological Changes

At a time of acute grief, a child's body responds to what the mind has been told. Among the more common physical symptoms a grieving child exhibits are:

- Tiredness, lack of energy
- Difficulty in sleeping, or sometimes excessive sleeping
- Lack of appetite or excessive appetite
- Tightness in the throat
- Shortness of breath
- General nervousness, trembling

- Headaches
- Stomach pain
- Loss of muscular strength
- Skin rashes

In most situations, adults can help the grieving child recognize that these physical "hurts" are quite normal and temporary, thereby lessening some of the child's concern. We also need to be aware that sometimes children unconsciously assume these "sick roles" in an effort to receive care for the emotional hurt. This happens most often in cases where the child isn't receiving adequate emotional support. In addition, it is not unusual for a child to identify with the physical symptoms that caused the death of the loved person. For example, if Dad died of a heart attack, the child may complain of chest pains.

The companion's helping role with physiological changes

- ***Remember that children's bodies respond to the stress of the death of someone loved.*** The aches and pains the child may complain of are often very real and they do hurt. The physical "hurts" a child expresses are often a form of emotional communication.

✻ ✻

Do children grieve differently than adults?

As I noted a number of years ago, "Grief does not focus on one's ability to understand but instead on one's ability to feel. Therefore any child mature enough to love is mature enough to grieve." Still, while children are quite capable of mourning, there are some distinctions between child and adult grief:

- A child's world is primarily a world of play.
- A child mourns in "doses"—or on an intermittent basis.
- Cognitive development affects a child's capacity to integrate the finality, inevitability and irreversibility of death.
- Children are more at the mercy of those around them for help or hindrance.
- Children don't want to be different from their peers (particularly teens).

✻ ✻

- **Don't punish or shame kids for seemingly unfounded feelings of illness.** When children feel shut off from avenues of emotional expression of their fears, questions, and concerns, the frequent consequence is that they become physically ill. The child unconsciously reasons, "If I can't play it out, act it out, or talk it out, I'll get sick—and then maybe I'll get nurtured!"

  Keep in mind that the child who is sick as a result of unexpressed thoughts and feelings does not consciously want to be sick—and certainly does not feel in control of her illness. We would not want to punish or shame a child for these physical expressions of grief.

- **Stay conscious of any pre-existing conditions (illness, injury, hospitalization) in the grieving child.** To experience bereavement on top of these types of losses often creates normal feelings of physical vulnerability and malaise. A child with concerns about his own physical well-being ("Will I die, too?") will often express these concerns indirectly through preoccupation with the well-being of others, as well: "Mommy, are you sick?" can mean, "Mommy, are you going to die, too?"

- **An excellent standard of care is to have any child you counsel get a good general medical examination.** This will often provide the child, other concerned adults, and you with reassuring information about the child's physical health. Occasionally, something that needs appropriate medical intervention will be found. A companioning approach to counseling bereaved children is a holistic one.

- **You will sometimes see transient forms of identification with the person who died through physical illness.** A child whose father died of cancer may complain of cancer "symptoms." A child whose sibling died of a brain tumor may complain of a headache. These are generally natural ways of identifying with and expressing longing for the person who died. Again, a physical exam is the best standard of care and often reassures the child as well as adults in the life of the child.

"Mommy, please don't go to work today!"
Dimension 3. Regression

When they're under the psychological stress of grief, children often want to return to the complete sense of protection and security they felt earlier in life. Among the more common regressive behaviors of childhood bereavement are the following:

- Over-dependence on a parent to the point of declining to go outside to play as they have done in the past.

- Desire to be nursed or rocked as they were at an earlier stage of development.

- Desire to sleep with a parent.

- An unwillingness to separate from a parent for any length of time.

- Desire to have others perform tasks for them that they are able to do for themselves, such as tying shoes, getting dressed, being fed and so forth.

- Refusal to work independently in the school setting and/or demanding constant individual attention and demonstrating dependent behaviors to the teacher and peers.

- Taking on a "sick role" in an effort to avoid attending school.

- Regression to talking "baby talk" and in general presenting themselves in an infant-like manner.

- Breakdown in the ability to function adequately in peer relationships.

Typically, regressive behaviors in grieving kids are temporary (although they sometimes last for months, even years, after a death) and pass as the child receives support in the journey through grief. Unfortunately, our society often perceives regressive behaviors as a total lack of self-control and discourages (or even punishes) both adults and children for displaying them.

When regressive behaviors continue for long periods of time, however, other factors may have complicated the child's grief response. On occasion, parents or other significant adults in the child's life actually reinforce or encourage this dependence. Why? Because adults experiencing grief themselves often feel guilty about not providing enough support to their children. They may attempt to compensate for this (real or false) sense of neglect by overprotecting or overindulging the child. Consequently, the child is kept in a dependent position as a result of the adult's need to feel in control of both the child and the situation.

Regressive behaviors can surface at any time during the grief process; however, they tend to be demonstrated to a greater extent within the first one to two years after the death. Typically, I view **continued** regressive behaviors as a barometer of emotional needs that are either not being met in a healthy, loving manner or, on the other hand, as an indication that adults in the child's life are attempting to meet their own needs through their child's behaviors.

The companion's helping role with regression

- *Allow the regressing grieving child to retreat to this safer, less complex time; this behavior is natural after the death of someone loved.* Regressive behaviors in a bereaved child are usually temporary and pass as he is supported in his grief journey. Note, too, that though these behaviors tend to be most noticeable in the first year or two after a death, a return to prior developmental levels can take place at any time during the child's grief experience.

- *Remember that demonstrating regressive behaviors may fill a significant need in the grieving child's life. Be patient and understanding.* Temporary, self-preserving regression undoubtedly serves a useful purpose for many bereaved children. It signals a need to be cared for, nurtured, and loved. It may also represent an attempt to return to a time in life before the trauma of the loss. The child may even see it as a way to retrieve the person who died.

- *Try to understand the unmet need underlying the behavior.* If a grieving nine-year-old tells you she's been staying home from school because she isn't ready to return to schoolwork yet, you might involve the girl's parents or guardians in several counseling sessions to sort out the causes of this behavior.

- *Provide a trusting, supportive presence for the child.* This suggestion stands no matter what the child's behavior. For children, to regress is simply to ask for care from the adults around them.

"What's happening to me?"
Dimension 4. Disorganization and Panic

A feeling bereaved children have that often occurs suddenly and unpredictably is a heightened sense of disorganization and panic. A wave of overwhelming thoughts and feelings makes the child wonder, "Who is going to take care of me now? Will our family survive? Will I survive?" At times children may feel as if they are out of touch with the ordinary proceedings of life, and many children become frightened by the duration and intensity of their feelings.

During this time the child often confronts both good and bad memories from the past. For example, while the child receives comfort from remembering the sound of Mom's voice, it is also painful. And then at other times the child may *want* to remember experiences and memories and finds doing so impossible. While this loss of memory is normal, it can be very scary to the child who doesn't understand it.

During this phase of grief the child may dream of the person who died, appear restless and irritable, seem unable to concentrate, or experience a disruption in normal eating and sleeping patterns. The child may seem hypersensitive and cry over things that seem totally unrelated to the death.

The companion's helping role with disorganization and panic

- ***Remember that these thoughts and feelings of disorganization and panic may ebb and flow for months, even years after the death.*** What children need most during this time is the constant physical presence of someone they trust. They also often need physical contact (hand-holding, hugging, caressing) to assure them of the caregiving that is and will continue to be extended to them. They need to be reassured about the naturalness of their feelings and behaviors, which in other circumstances would be considered highly unusual.

- ***During this time the child may also have a real need to cry, talk, or play out their grief.*** The role of the adult caregiver is not to interrupt with false reassurances, but to let crying and talking take their natural course. (Most children don't cry for more than 2-3 minutes at a time, even though it seems longer to us adults.) At times the content of what the child says may make little sense, but that's OK—it will still help him feel better. In moving through and being supported during this frightening part of grief, children are capable of turning grief into growth and pain into gain.

- ***Remember that disorientation in grief precedes reorientation.*** Practice being patient with the child and keep in mind you are a caregiver, not a curegiver. Be aware that many children work through disorientation and panic through repetitive play and activities. Watch for the symbolism in the play that often reflects needs for safety and security. Repetitive play is often a form of "telling the story" and is developmentally appropriate for children as they do the work of mourning.

- *The thoughts, feelings, and behaviors of this dimension of grief do not come all at once and are often experienced in a wave-like fashion.* The child may one day appear to be "fine" and the next day experiencing disorganization or panic. Again, this is normal and remembering this will help the child to feel safe with you. The child may teach you and other adults that they don't need a lot of words from you, but instead non-verbal forms of support like eye contact, gestures of care, and a willingness to play with them.

"I hate you!"
Dimension 5. Explosive Emotions

A child's explosive emotions—including not just anger but feelings of hate, blame, terror, resentment, rage, and jealousy—can be upsetting and threatening to adults because they are often uncertain how to respond.

Explosive emotions often express a child's desire to restore things to the way they were before the death. Anger and other related emotions are a grieving child's natural, intelligent response to the death of someone loved and an effort to restore a valued relationship that has been lost.

Explosive emotions may also signal a grieving child's anger at the person who died because, as the child views the situation, "If Daddy loved me enough, he wouldn't have died and left me." The child may then further reason, "If Dad doesn't love me, no one can love me. There must be something about me that makes me unlovable."

A bereaved child's rage may be directed toward anyone available: a surviving parent, a teacher, playmates, God, or the world in general. Through this behavior, some grieving kids may even be testing the idea that they should never love again. The rationale: If they love anyone again, that person may die, too.

The fact that the dead person does not come back, despite the child's explosive emotions, is actually a part of the reality testing necessary for eventual healing to occur. As the child gradually becomes aware that the person who died will not return, these explosive emotions will typically soften.

My companioning experiences with hundreds of bereaved children have taught me one final, fundamental lesson about explosive emotions: there is a healthy survival value in being able to temporarily protest the painful reality of the loss. Having the capacity to express anger gives a child the courage to survive during a difficult time. Children who do not receive permission to do so may slide into chronic depression. They are literally deprived of a means of psychological survival.

Adults tend to be intolerant of explosive emotions because we reason, "If the child is angry at me, something must be wrong with either him or me." And so we discourage the anger, the rage. Our children in turn see how uncomfortable we are with their anger and they may begin to feel guilty about it.

Unfortunately, grieving children who repress or deny their explosive feelings will turn their anger inward. The painful results are low self-esteem, depression, chronic feelings of guilt, and physical complaints.

The companion's helping role with explosive emotions

The major role of caring adults when a child demonstrates explosive emotions is to be a supportive stabilizer. Adults need to tolerate, encourage, and validate explosive emotions without judging, retaliating, or arguing.

A word of caution: Never attempt to prescribe what these emotions should be for a bereaved child. Simply be alert for them. Let the child teach you if explosive emotions are part of his grief experience. In some cases, such as when a death is anticipated due to terminal illness, the demonstration of explosive emotions may be mild or nonexistent.

- *Encourage the healthy expression of a child's explosive emotions so these feelings will be expressed, not repressed.* If you simply listen and watch as the child demonstrates her anger, she will come to understand that her feelings are accepted. When she has calmed down, you might also ask her why she thinks she is feeling so angry; if she can't offer an explanation that will help her understand her explosive emotions, perhaps you can.

- *Remember that explosive emotional behavior often signals the child's underlying feelings of pain, helplessness, frustration, fear, and hurt.* During this difficult time, caring adults need to "be with" and support the grieving child as he does the painful work of mourning.

- *Provide alternate outlets for expression of anger.* During counseling sessions, you can encourage children to express their anger through shadow boxing, pillow fighting, and other physical activities. You might also ask them to paint their anger or write about it. In using these techniques, you are not only learning about the child's anger, you are teaching her constructive ways to deal with her anger.

"I got in a fight at school today."
Dimension 6. Acting-Out

Many children express the pain of grief through acting-out. This behavior usually varies depending on the child's age and developmental level. The child may become unusually loud and noisy, have a temper outburst, start fights with other children, defy authority, or simply rebel against everything. Other examples of acting-out behavior include getting poor grades in school or assuming a general attitude that says, "I don't care about anything." Older children may even run away from home.

Understanding and appropriately responding to the grieving child's acting out may seem a daunting task. But when broken down into its component parts, it is not so overwhelming. To begin, it is important to understand why bereaved children act out in the first place. A number of factors influence this behavior.

Feelings of insecurity—Grieving children naturally experience a sense of insecurity following the death of someone loved. After all, when it is a family member who has died, the child's most stabilizing influence—the family—has been disturbed. Acted-out feelings unconsciously provide the child with a sense of control and power.

While temper outbursts don't resolve the child's anxiety, they do provide a way for the child to feel she has regained some control. Tantrums or fighting also frighten others around the child, adding to the bereaved child's feelings of power.

Feelings of abandonment—Grieving children may feel as if their dead parent has abandoned or "died on them." Consequently, they sometimes feel unloved; their self-esteem is affected. As a result, some bereaved children will act out to create a self-fulfilling prophecy: "See, nobody loves me."

A desire to provoke punishment—Even though it is not rational to adults, some grieving children reason that, "If I'm so bad that somebody I loved died, then I deserve to be punished." Again, this reasoning is usually an unconscious process.

When it is a parent who died—especially the parent who was the family's primary disciplinarian—the child may act out in an attempt to get the parent to "come back" and mete out punishment. The rationale: "If I'm bad, Dad will have to come back and make me behave."

Protection from future losses—Grieving children sometimes initiate rejection in an effort to prevent feelings of "abandonment" in the future. Their acting-out behaviors serve to keep people at a distance. The result—they become the ones who control the situation rather than passively suffer the possibility of being left again.

Essentially, the bereaved child unconsciously reasons that it is better to be the abandoner than the abandoned. Acting-out behavior protects the child from intimate relationships and the additional hurt and pain of a future loss.

Demonstration of internal feelings of grief—As I have said, many children grieve but do not mourn. When this happens, feelings build up inside the child with no way to be expressed outwardly. Ultimately, the stress erupts—often in the form of acting-out behaviors.

The companion's helping role with acting out

- ***Understand the needs that underlie the acting-out behaviors.***
  Acting-out in bereaved children is often an indirect, unconscious cry for help, so adults must work to understand what function the acting-out behavior serves. Caregivers should first ask themselves, "What are the genuine needs of a grieving child who acts out?"

  But being aware of this phenomenon does not mean you should ignore it. Caregivers must still set appropriate limits while at the same time recognizing the possible reasons for the child's actions. My experience as a grief counselor has shown me that the two greatest needs of a bereaved child are for affection and a sense of security. Appropriate limit-setting and discipline, then, should attempt to meet these essential needs. We must let grieving kids know that we love them despite their present behavior.

- ***Set limits without demonstrating anger or using violence.***
  Too often, bereaved children are punished in ways that are counterproductive. Discipline and limit-setting must communicate to the child that adults accept and love the child despite the misbehavior. Unfortunately, some adults attempt to set limits on acting-out behavior while communicating to the child that he or she is a "bad boy" or "bad girl." The message often is, "You are

being punished because you are bad." No distinction is made between inappropriate behavior and being a bad person.

- ***Recognize that adult discipline will eventually lead to self-discipline.*** Adult modeling and reasonable boundary-setting help grieving children develop their internal controls while at the same time providing them the opportunity to make painful mistakes. As we all know, discovering we make mistakes as we grow up is an important lesson.

"I'm the man of the house now."
Dimension 7. Hyper-maturity

The opposite of regressive behavior on the part of the bereaved child is hyper-maturity. This is when the child attempts to grow up very quickly and become the "man" or "woman" of the house, often in an effort to replace a dead parent. In my past writings I have referred to this tendency as the "Big Man" or "Big Woman" Syndrome.

An example: ***Amy's mother died six months ago, and Amy and her father have been working through their grief.*** However, Amy's father said to a friend, "My daughter Amy, who is only ten years old, tries to be just like her mother was. She has been trying to cook all of the meals and insists that she sits where her mother did at the kitchen table....She cleans the house in the same order and manner of my wife....She waits at the door when I return from work and asks me about my day in exactly the same words my wife used for years."

Grieving children act over-mature for a variety of reasons. This girl's attempt to take on her mother's role may be a symbolic way of keeping Mom alive. Or, it could be another way for her to protect herself from a common sense of hopelessness and helplessness. She probably also thinks that filling in for Mom makes Dad feel better, too.

Many times, though, bereaved children don't dream up this behavior all by themselves. Adults encourage them by saying things like, "You're the oldest, Ben. You'll have to be the man of the house now," or, "You'll need to take care of the other kids now that your Mom is gone." Some adults also encourage this hyper-mature behavior because they simply feel more comfortable dealing with "adult-acting" kids. And a surviving parent may actually, consciously or unconsciously, attempt to have the child replace the dead parent.

Regardless of the cause, hyper-maturity is dangerous for grieving children because it doesn't allow them to deal with their grief at their own developmental levels. In fact, it tends to displace grief because the suddenly grown-up children focus on their difficult new roles instead of on their normal thoughts and feelings.

The companion's helping role with hyper-maturity

- *Remember that children in single parent families often naturally mature more quickly due to the economic and social realities of this lifestyle.* While we as caregivers need to understand this reality, we must also encourage same-age peer contact and help the family to understand the normalcy of this. Don't shame families in which the children are of necessity hyper-mature, but rather help them understand the behavior and respond appropriately to it.

- *Keep in mind that well-meaning adults sometimes encourage this forced sense of maturity on a grieving child because they find it easier to respond to the child at this inappropriate level.* If this occurs, a systems approach to helping the family is often useful. Again, be conscious not to prematurely confront or shame families; join them before you move them. Often, this hyper-maturity isn't something they have consciously set in motion. As a matter of fact, at a societal level, it is often a projection of messages to "put things behind you and go on" (in other words, "grow up"). Actually, the bereaved child and family need to go into neutral before they can get into gear. When we companion, our task is often to help them compassionately slow down, not speed up!

- *Be aware of the potential negative impact that trite comments can have on a grieving child.* We can help educate well-intentioned but misinformed adults about not handing out clichéd, damaging advice such as, "Now you have to be the man of the house." The goal should be to work to help bereaved children and their families experience as normal as possible maturational and development patterns following the death of someone loved. A difficult but achievable task!

"I'm so scared."

Dimension 8. Fear

Grieving children often feel afraid. When the reality begins to set in that the parent or other significant person in the child's life will not be coming back, it is not unusual for the child to become frightened. During these times children may ask themselves, "If one parent dies, will the other?" or "Sophie left us, will Jenna die, too?"

Frequently, the underlying fear is that there will be no one left to take care of them. This fear often is increased when the child witnesses a surviving parent struggling with his or her own grief. The parent may seem detached from the child's world and appear incapable of caring for the child. Related to this experience is the child's fear of watching people whom they love grieve. Parents and other adults around the child must reassure her that she is loved and will be cared for.

Another common fear of the grieving child is the fear of loving again. Children may reason that if they had not loved the dead person so much, they would not be experiencing the pain of this grief.

Helping children understand and accept these feelings will help them cope. Children can be helped to understand that giving and receiving love are two of the greatest gifts of life. Often children have difficulty understanding that the pain of grief is part of life, living, and loving. However, the presence of caring adults can make a true difference in a child's ability to cope with many fears.

Another common fear that many bereaved children experience is the fear of their own death. They may be frightened at the slightest hint of illness or secretly feel that they too will soon die. Again, the child needs reassurance and the loving support of adult caregivers.

The companion's helping role with fear

- *Be sensitive to a child's fears.* For example, children's questions related to an adult truly caring about them are frequently an attempt to determine if they can count on the adult not to leave or to die. Accepting children's questions and fears means you accept each child—critical because grieving children can be extremely sensitive to the slightest hint of rejection. Also recognize that underneath expressions of fear is the emotional need for warmth, acceptance, and understanding.

- *Use the "wishes and fears inventory" with the child.* This is where you ask the child to tell you three wishes and three fears. Having expressed some wishes (a task most children are used to), children often go right into fears they might be concealing. This is only one of many ways you might learn from a child about fears he or she might be experiencing. Be creative; do what seems to work for you.

- *Go fishing.* With proper timing and pacing, you simply say to the child, "Some kids have taught me that when someone in their life dies it can be pretty scary. It there anything that's scary to you?" Sensing your desire to understand, they will often go on to teach you about their unique fears.

"It's my fault Uncle Jim died."
Dimension 9. Guilt

It is very human for both adults and children to blame themselves when someone they love dies. For children this can be an especially tough struggle because they have particular difficulty understanding cause-effect relationships.

Young children are susceptible to "magical thinking"; they believe that by thinking about something they can make it happen. What child, for example, hasn't wished his parents would go away and leave him alone? So when a parent dies, the child may well assume blame and feel guilty for thinking these thoughts. The child may blame himself for any number of things, ranging from being bad to having had angry feelings toward the person who died. The child may even take total responsibility for the death, yet say nothing to anyone about this feeling. If adults are not perceptive and aware of this phenomenon, it may well go unnoticed.

This dimension of guilt may be revealed when the child says things like, "If only I would have...," or "I wish I could have...," or, "Why didn't I...." Self-defeating thoughts and behaviors often mount as the grieving child experiences feelings of guilt. Frequently, a guilt-wracked child feels helpless and worthless. The child may say to herself, "I am a bad person for what I have done (or not done)."

In fact, bereaved children who feel responsible for the death of someone loved often think that they will be punished in some way and may actually seek out forms of self-punishment. This sense that something bad will happen may become a self-fulfilling prophecy.

Moreover, when children feel helpless, they may attempt to gain some sense of control by thinking that if they would have done something differently, the person they loved would not have died. In other words, if they see themselves as being the cause of the death, they think there may well be something they could do to bring the person back to life. The child may say, "If you come back I'll be good; I'll never be noisy again or make you get up early with me." This kind of thinking is at times reinforced in those families where someone is always to blame for whatever happens.

Survival guilt and relief—Surviving a person who has died, particularly a parent, brother or sister, can generate feelings of guilt in grieving kids. The child may observe the other parent's pain and reasons, "Maybe it should have been me instead of my father." What the child may not realize is that if he or she had died, the parent would be experiencing the same pain of grief.

Relief-guilt syndrome—Another type of guilt may evolve when a person's death brings a child some sense of relief or release. This situation often occurs when the person who died had been ill for a long time or the child's relationship with the person who died was in conflict.

After a long illness, a child may not miss the frequent trips to the hospital or the family's ongoing focus on the dying person. If the bereaved child is not able to acknowledge this sense of relief as natural and not equal to a lack of love, he or she may feel guilty for feeling relieved.

Personality factors and guilt—Another form of guilt evolves from long-standing personality factors within the grieving child. Some children are taught early in life that when anything bad or unfortunate occurs, it is their fault. Consequently, when a death occurs, they look first within themselves to find blame. This kind of guilt becomes an ingrained part of their character development.

These children definitely need the context of a professional counseling relationship to make constructive changes. Unfortunately, these children often live in families where outside help is not made available.

Guilt and punishment—Some bereaved children anticipate that punishment (from outside or inside) should result from experiencing feelings of guilt. As a consequence, adults might see children attempting to lessen their guilt through punishment. They may directly or indirectly ask to be punished.

Obviously, seeking out punishment is self-destructive and only makes the child's situation worse. For caring adults, the task is to help the grieving child feel less guilty and thus reduce his or her need to demonstrate self-destructive behaviors. These children are often also accident-prone and exhibit a high level of risk-taking behavior.

Joy-guilt syndrome—A bereaved child can also experience feelings of guilt when he or she begins to re-experience any kind of joy or happiness in life. These feelings often stem from a sense of loyalty to the person who died and a fear that being happy in some way betrays that relationship. Opportunities to explore these feelings are necessary as the child moves forward in his or her grief experience.

The companion's helping role with guilt

- *Foremost, we must provide opportunities for the child to talk and play out the circumstances surrounding the death.* Try to prevent adults around the child from reinforcing the thought that death is a form of punishment. As the child recalls memories, either good or bad, talk about them openly and honestly. Help the child understand that being angry or upset with a person does not cause the person to die. The child can be helped to understand that at times it is normal for people to get angry with people they care about. The bereaved child also can be helped to understand that we cannot control certain things in life.

- *In the case of the child who is too young to articulate thoughts and feelings, the sense of a trusting relationship with an adult figure is paramount.* Adults are capable of expressing a sense of warmth and acceptance through nonverbal as well as verbal means. Just as children learn to be able to give love by being loved, they learn self-acceptance by being accepted. For the verbal child the opportunity to participate in a permissive, patient, and non-judgmental conversation often allows for the opportunity to work through feelings of guilt.

- *Go slowly in working through guilt with children.* First, work to enter into what they think and feel in an effort to understand. What is their phenomenological reality? As adults, we are sometimes quick to want to take away a child's feelings in general, but particularly guilt. Yet, if children feel guilty, they feel guilty— we cannot and should not try to save them from this feeling.

- *Be alert to some children's conscious or unconscious need to punish themselves because of feelings of guilt.* Self-punishment themes in children may be illustrated through inappropriate risk-taking, accident-proneness, chronic depression, and general self-neglect. These types of behaviors demand immediate help from caring adults.

"I'm glad Grandma died."
Dimension 10. Relief

At times, a grieving child very appropriately experiences a sense of relief when someone in her life dies. Death can bring relief from suffering, especially when due to a long and debilitating illness. The bereaved child's sense of relief is an emotion that is frequently overlooked, misunderstood, or repressed by adults. When adults do not allow (and therefore do not help the child understand) this emotion, the child may feel guilty. Children may think they are the only ones who feel relieved. The result is all too often a tremendous self-imposed attack on the child's self-esteem, potentially resulting in depression.

Grieving children may also experience a sense of relief due to their developmental stage. Egocentrism is normal in childhood, and when someone is ill in the family, the focus of attention is usually diverted toward the sick person. After the death, many children are naturally relieved because they think that now they will receive some of the attention they crave. Of course, we as adults should never blame or shame a child for this normal feeling.

Feelings of relief also relate to the reality that we as humans, regardless of age, do not begin to grieve and mourn at the moment of a terminally ill person's death. The experience of grief may begin when the person we love begins the transition from being alive and well to becoming unwell and dying. Herein lies the source of another potential complication for children: When the child is deceived about an illness or, worse yet, flat out lied to, she may have no knowledge that the person has even been ill. So, when the death occurs, what others may perceive as an anticipated death actually becomes a sudden, unexpected death for the child. Therefore, some adults might assume the child is relieved when in reality she has come to grief before she is prepared to mourn! This often occurs in closed family systems in which children are isolated from events impacting the family.

In an open-family system, I often witness a natural progression of anticipatory mourning that includes the children. This progression may occur as follows: what starts out as sense of "he is sick" becomes "he is very sick" becomes "he may die" becomes "he is going to die" becomes "he is suffering so much" becomes "I'll be glad when he is out of pain" toward "he is dead" which in turn opens the doorway to many other thoughts and feelings. Obviously, the child who is openly involved in this progression is more likely to express some aspects of relief when the death does come.

Death can also be experienced as relief when the child has been the victim of physical, emotional or sexual abuse by the person who died. The child may teach you she feels safe for this first time in her life. I also frequently witness relief in children when someone has died due to chemical abuse or dependence. They may have loved the person but not liked the fall-out consequences from the chemical abuse or dependence.

Regardless of the death circumstances it's caused by, relief is experienced not in isolation, but in tandem with a number of other emotions. Many children will be confronted with mourning not only what they lost, but what they wish they could have had in a relationship with this person. They may do more work on this as they grow into adulthood and do some catch-up mourning.

The companion's helping role with relief

- ***Remember that relief is often a normal response for the grieving child.*** Listen to or observe acceptingly the child's sense of relief without projecting shame or guilt.

- ***Keep in mind that relief does not necessarily equal a lack of love for the person who died.*** Actually, being relieved that someone is no longer suffering is a natural element of love.

- ***Do not prescribe relief, particularly in the period of time shortly after the death.*** The child and family are rarely, if ever, fully prepared for the moment of the death, even when the terminally ill person has been near death for some time. If the child should teach you that he feels immediate relief, so be it. However, when we companion, we do not prescribe feelings. We allow bereaved children to teach us what feelings are present and then respond to them.

"There's a big hole in my heart."
Dimension 11. Sadness

This dimension of grief is often the most difficult for grieving children. The full sense of loss and emptiness never takes place all at once, and as it begins to set in, sadness, emptiness, and feelings of depression often follow. These feelings often surface when the child really realizes that the dead person will not be coming back.

One difficulty with this sense of loss and emptiness is that it may take place long after adults in the child's life think grief support is necessary—typically months following the death. Children may wonder why they are crying more at this time than they did just after the death occurred.

As children struggle to come to terms with the finality and reality of the death, they very naturally become depressed. Of course, the death of a significant person in their life is something *about* which to be depressed. During this time the child may demonstrate:

- A lack of interest in self and others

- Change of appetite and sleeping patterns

- Prolonged withdrawal

- Nervousness

- Inability to experience pleasure

- Low self-esteem

The child may feel totally alone and empty, usually resulting in a heightening of these feelings. These characteristics of their mourning should change very slowly over time, assuming they have a "safe place" to mourn.

The child who is not in an environment conducive to recognizing and encouraging loss, emptiness, and sadness will sometimes feel unable to express these feelings. Suppressed feelings often push for release, while the child is encouraged to repress them. The frequent result is increased anxiety, agitation, and a sense of being emotionally and physically drained.

Obviously, the bereaved child is particularly vulnerable during this period. The child may actively seek a substitute for the person who died. Feelings of attachment can be displaced to the extent that a strong dependency upon another person occurs. The person to whom the child attaches often reminds the child—and us—of the person who died.

The companion's helping role with sadness

- ***Encourage the child to talk about his or her intense feelings of sadness.*** The regular presence of a supportive and stabilizing adult caregiver is helpful when the grieving child is feeling sad. While strong new attachments may appear to be helpful to the child at this time, continuing the work of grief is really the task at hand.

The child should be encouraged to talk about and/or play out intense feelings. An important person in the child's life has died, but that person still exists in the child's memory. The child should not be denied the opportunity to express these feelings and work them through.

- **Find creative ways for the child to express his sadness.** At times, bereaved children find it easier to express such intense feelings through play, artwork, or writing. Whatever helps the child to express and explore feelings should be respected. Don't be surprised that if during this dimension of grief the child wants to review the events preceding the death and the death itself. It is as if each time the child talks about the death it becomes a little more bearable.

- **Teach grieving kids about "griefbursts" so when they experience one, they'll be less frightened.** "Griefbursts"—sudden, unexpected, and strong feelings of sadness— can be extremely frightening to children. When companioning, helping means not allowing children to feel alone as they struggle with these feelings. Many children will not initiate talking about their grief attacks. They often, however, give indirect cues. When these urgent cues are not heard or are misunderstood, the result is often another experience of loss for the bereaved child.

✳ ✳ ✳ ✳ ✳ ✳ ✳ ✳ ✳ ✳ ✳ ✳
Signs of complicated mourning

- Total denial of the reality of the death
- Persistent panic, fear
- Prolonged physical complaints without organic findings
- Prolonged feelings of guilt or responsibility for the death when the child obviously isn't responsible. (Children who feel guilt because they *are* responsible for the death often benefit from individual counseling as well.)
- *Chronic* patterns of apathy and/or depression
- Chronic hostility, acting-out toward others or self
- Prolonged change in typical behavior patterns or personality (e.g. the amiable child who now gets in fights all the time or the normally outgoing child who becomes introverted and withdrawn.)
- Consistent withdrawal from friends and family members
- Dramatic, ongoing changes in sleeping and eating patterns
- Drug or alcohol abuse
- Suicidal thoughts or actions

✳ ✳ ✳ ✳ ✳ ✳ ✳ ✳ ✳ ✳ ✳ ✳

"I miss Mom, but I'm going to be OK."
Dimension 12. Reconciliation

In many grief models, the final "stage" of bereavement is referred to as resolution. Other paradigms use the terms recovery, re-establishment

✳ ✳

Normal grief or clinical depression?

- In normal grief, children respond to comfort and support; clinically depressed children often reject support.

- The grieving child is often able to use play to work out feelings of grief; the depressed child is more often resistant to the use of play.

- The bereaved child is often openly angry; the depressed child may complain and be irritable, but may not directly express anger.

- Grieving children will usually connect depressed feelings to the death; depressed children often do not relate their feelings to any life event.

- In normal grief, bereaved children can still experience moments of enjoyment in life; depressed children often project a pervasive sense of doom.

- Caring adults around the grieving child can sense feelings of sadness and emptiness; the depressed child often projects a sense of hopelessness and chronic emptiness.

- While the bereaved child is more likely to have transient physical complaints, the depressed child may have chronic physical complaints.

- Grieving children may express guilt over some aspect of the loss; depressed children often have generalized feelings of guilt.

- While the self-esteem of bereaved children is temporarily impacted, it is usually not the deep loss of esteem typically seen in clinically depressed children.

✳ ✳

or reorganization. The problem with these definitions is that people—children and adults alike—do not "get over" grief. My personal and professional experience tells me that a total return to "normalcy" after the death of someone loved is not possible; everyone is changed by the experience of grief. Recovery, as it is often understood by mourners and caregivers, is erroneously seen as an absolute, a perfect state of re-establishment.

Reconciliation is a term I find more appropriate for what occurs as the grieving person works to integrate the new reality of moving forward in life without the physical presence of the person who has died. With reconciliation comes a renewed sense of energy and confidence, an ability to fully acknowledge the reality of the death, and a capacity to become re-involved in the activities of living. There is also an acknowledgment that pain and grief are difficult yet necessary parts of life.

The bereaved child's reconciliation after a death *is a process, not an event*. Adults should avoid using specific timetables with specific points at which a child should "be over" grief. Human beings never get over our grief, but instead become reconciled to it. Caregivers who allow and encourage children to move toward their grief, instead of away from it, aid in this reconciliation process.

Among the changes often noted during the child's reconciliation process are:

- A return to stable eating and sleeping patterns
- A renewed sense of energy and well-being
- A subjective sense of release from the person who has died
- Increased thinking and judgment-making capabilities
- The capacity to enjoy life experiences
- A recognition of the reality and finality of the death
- The establishment of new and healthy relationships

Perhaps the most important gain for the child in this reconciliation process is the discovery of the ability to cope successfully with the loss. This coping is achieved only with the assistance of caring adults.

The companion's helping role with reconciliation

- *If we are able to recognize that grief is a complex set of emotions that vary from child to child, we can be more open and honest in helping young people cope with death and achieve reconciliation.* Grief is not something a child should be ashamed of or try to hide. Only because children give and receive love are they able to grieve and grow. As caregivers, we must model the giving and receiving of love as we interact with the child.

- *In a very real sense, grief is a privilege for both children and adults.* We have a capacity for deep feelings that lower forms of life are not able to experience and appreciate. Only because we have the capacity to love do we grieve. When children are born into this world, they do not have the choice of feeling or not feeling. The capacity to feel is innate. However, we do have the choice as to how open and honest we will be about our feelings and how committed we will be to helping both ourselves and our children in working through these feelings in a healthy, life-affirming manner.

- **We must understand grief as an integral part of life and living and must work to reverse the trend toward protecting children from grief.** Therefore, if the material shared in this chapter stimulates discussion, raises questions, and increases one's sense of hope, it will have served a most useful purpose.

✳ ✳ ✳

Feeling all this grief is hard work for a child. The more open she stays to her feelings and expresses herself, the more able she will be to move from grief to mourning. The following chapter discusses how the grieving child reconciles her grief.

Chapter Four

How the Grieving Child Heals: The Six Reconciliation Needs of Mourning

So far we have examined several aspects of childhood grief. We have reviewed the influences on a child's mourning (what I've also called "mourning styles") and the ways in which those mourning styles are manifested through a child's behaviors, thoughts, and feelings. In the Prologue and Introduction, we also explored my grief gardening model and what it can mean for a child to grow through grief.

But how does a grieving child mourn his way from the starting point of his grief—which is largely a factor of mourning style influences—through his many thoughts and feelings to the destination of reconciliation and growth? Asked more simply, how *does* the bereaved child heal?

I believe the grieving child heals, over time, when her mourning needs are consistently met. For a flower to grow, the plant must receive adequate nutrients from the soil, ample water, and sufficient sun. It also needs protection from pests, disease, and invasive weeds. The gardener who understands and helps his plants meet these needs will be rewarded with a lush, healthy garden.

Bereaved children have equally fundamental needs that must be met if they are to heal and grow. This chapter defines what I term "the six reconciliation needs of mourning." Others have labeled these the *tasks* of childhood mourning. As a grief companion, you probably know intuitively what a child's mourning needs are, but you may never have analyzed and articulated them in this manner. I find that doing so helps me better understand each child's grief journey and my role as his companion.

Need 1. Acknowledge the reality of the death.

Before he can move on in his grief journey, the bereaved child must be helped to gently confront the reality that someone he loves has died and will not return.

Of course, children must be provided with an open and honest explanation (at their level of developmental understanding) about the nature and cause of the death if they are to meet this mourning need. As caring adults, we must openly share clear information about the death with the affected children. Remember, kids can cope with what they know. They cannot cope with what they don't know.

We as a society must work to overcome our instinct to protect children from sad news. We must also refrain from thinking that children are "too young to understand." Perhaps they are too young to fully understand everything about the death, but they are never too young to feel.

The news of a death is best conveyed by someone close to the child. When possible, it shouldn't come from someone who doesn't have a pre-existing, stabilizing relationship with the child. Keep in mind the importance of eye contact, a comforting tone of voice, and appropriate physical comfort that conveys security. Be certain to avoid euphemisms such as "sleep" and "passed away," which will only confuse the child.

As a counselor, of course, you more often see children who have already been told about a death. So, while at times you may not be able to influence the way in which children first hear about the death of someone loved, you can help explain what death means. If a child teaches you that she doesn't understand what death is all about, explain that the dead person's body has stopped working and it will never again work the way it used to. The person's body will not see or hear and won't talk, move, or breathe anymore. The body won't feel cold or hot or be happy or sad. When a person's body dies, the person doesn't feel anything anymore. These kinds of explanations help the child understand that the person who died cannot come back. Being supportive of the child as she gently confronts this new reality is a vital part of helping with this reconciliation need of mourning.

Remember, do not expect that the child's acknowledgment of the reality will be similar to an adult's response. Many children naturally respond to news of death with indifference or an apparent lack of feelings. This is the child's natural way of protecting himself; he will embrace the full reality of the death only intermittently, in doses. A lack of outward mourning does not mean that children are not moving toward the reality—they are just doing it in their own way and time.

Many times a bereaved child asks questions that are prompted by this need to acknowledge the reality of the death. Do not try to attach adult meanings to the child's questions, which are usually quite simple and factual. The questions they ask and re-ask are one of the central ways in which they embrace the full reality of death.

The ability to acknowledge the reality of the death only comes about after the child is provided with opportunities to talk out, play out, and even act out the circumstances of the death. Typically, the child does not embrace the full sense of loss until several months after the death. (Meeting this need can take *years* if the child has been told half-truths or even out-and-out lied to about the reality of the death.) Prior to that, the child will likely, consciously and unconsciously, work to distance himself from the pain that is part and parcel of meeting this critical first mourning need.

For the adult companion, the art of helping meet this need lies in balancing the child's need to acknowledge this new reality with the child's normal desire to push the reality away. As we learn to companion children in grief—and not to push or pull them through the experience—we become capable of being true grief gardeners. We become available to the child not only with our heads, but with our hearts.

Need 2. Move toward the pain of the loss while being nurtured physically, emotionally, and spiritually.

To heal, the grieving child must be not just allowed but encouraged to embrace the wide range of thoughts and feelings that result from the death.

This task is often complicated by adults who want to protect the child from the impact of the death. This tendency is understandable, but in prematurely moving the child away from the hurts of grief, well-intentioned but misinformed adults can interfere with the child's healing and may even cause long-term harm.

The desire of many adults to "spare children" is often caused by their own feelings of discomfort, fear, or anxiety. The reasoning? If adults can get the child to avoid feelings of pain and hurt, they won't have to "be with" the child in the grief journey. The sad reality is that many adults will try to protect themselves from pain by protecting children from pain.

As we companion, we must be careful not to blame or shame those adults who have adopted this overprotective stance. After all, they have grown up in a culture in which the role of pain is misunderstood. In our society, to feel and express thoughts and feelings (or in a child's situation, to play or act out these feelings) connected to loss is often considered unnecessary and inappropriate. Mourning makes us uncomfortable. Yet, in reality, it is in moving toward our hurts that we ultimately heal.

So, to heal from losses in our culture takes tremendous courage, particularly for children. Why? Because many children must overcome adult behaviors such as isolation, deception, and overprotection from the events surrounding death.

The art of helping bereaved children with this need is to allow them to teach you how they feel. You cannot prod children into this, but you can work to create a safe, nurturing environment where they sense your desire to understand.

Grieving children need permission to mourn. Sometimes what they need most from adults is an awareness that it is OK to talk out and play out their many thoughts and feelings. If the suffering is avoided, denied, or repressed by adults surrounding bereaved children, those very children will be abandoned at a time when they most need the presence of loving adults. Actually, it's not really a question of, "Will the child feel or not feel?" It is a question of, "When he feels, will he be able to express himself in the companionship of loving adults?"

If we are to be those loving adults, we must also be careful not to project to grieving kids that they will (or should) feel exactly as we do about death. So, while the child must move toward whatever feelings he experiences, keep in mind that these feelings can be, and often are, very different from our own grief feelings.

We must also remember that children mourn intermittently, moving at times toward and then away from the depth of the loss. Respecting children means understanding this wave-like quality in their capacity to mourn. This also means remaining available as a stabilizing presence long after the event of the death.

Note, too, that moving toward the pain of the loss is just one facet of this reconciliation need. The child's simultaneous need to be nurtured physically, emotionally, and spiritually is the other facet. Physically, the child needs adequate nutrition and hydration, daily rest, and regular physical activity. Her emotional needs are many, but at bottom what she needs is a safe psychological environment and a nurturing support system that assures her she is loved and cared for. And the bereaved child's spiritual needs include such things as embracing "meaning of life" issues in the face of death.

Need 3. Convert the relationship with the person who has died from one of presence to one of memory.

This reconciliation need involves allowing and encouraging the child to move from the "here and now" of his relationship with the person who died to the "what was." Though the grieving child should not be expected to give up all ties to the person who died (actually it is unwise and often damaging to communicate to the child that any and all relationships with the person who died are over), there must be an alteration of the relationship from one of presence to one of memory.

Precious memories, occasional dreams reflecting the significance of the relationship, and living legacies are among the manifestations of this different form of a continued relationship. The process of beginning to embrace memories often begins with the funeral. Unfortunately, there are some adults who prevent children from this vital part of the work of mourning by excluding them from the funeral. Remembering the person who has died through the funeral helps affirm the value of the life that was lived.

In fact, the memories that families share during this time often set the tone for the changed nature of the relationship. The funeral ritual encourages the expression of cherished memories and allows for both tears and laughter. Memories that were made in love can be gently embraced in the companionship of loving adults.

Remembering can be a very slow, painful, and incremental process. When children are particularly hurting from the sting of grief, nonjudgmental support and understanding may be what is most needed. However, sometimes we must encourage the gentle encountering of memories. Stimulating the child to keep memories alive rather than blocking them out helps affirm the value of the relationship.

In a culture where many people do not understand the value and function of memories, most bereaved children will need help meeting this important mourning need. There are many ways you can help grieving children with memory work. A few examples are noted below:

- Modeling the expression of your own feelings and memories.
- Encouraging the child to teach you about some of her own memories.
- Providing the child with keepsakes that belonged to the person who died.

- Allowing the child to be involved in the funeral ritual.

- Talking about experiences the child had with the person who died.

- Displaying photos of the person who died.

- Visiting places of special significance that stimulate memories.

- Naturally bringing up the person who died in conversations with the child.

- Reviewing photo albums together at special times like holidays, birthdays, and anniversaries.

- Keeping in mind any major milestones that might create occasions for reminiscing, e.g. graduating from grade school to middle school, the child's own birthday, etc.

Perhaps one of the best ways to embrace memories is through the creation of a "Memory Book"—a scrapbook containing photos, mementos, letters, reflective writings, etc. that commemorate the person who died. This scrapbook will often become a valued collection of memories that the child will call upon often during her grief journey.

Special mention should be made of children with ambivalent memories, particularly those children whose memories are marked by emotional, physical, or sexual abuse. These kinds of experiences make it naturally difficult to openly embrace memories. These children need nonjudgmental adults they trust enough to explore these painful memories with. Obviously, these kinds of memories complicate the task of mourning and require your special professional attention. Children who are not helped to place these memories in perspective (and helped to understand that they were victims) may carry an underlying sadness or anger into their adult lives.

My experience in learning from thousands of bereaved children is that remembering makes hoping possible. Grieving children's futures become open to new experiences and relationships to the extent that past memories have been embraced.

Need 4. Develop a new self-identity based on a life without the person who died.

Among the most difficult changes the bereaved child encounters are those that reflect his or her personal identity. Personal identity or self-perception comes from the ongoing process of establishing a sense of who one is. The death of someone loved can, and often does, permanently change the child's self-perception.

Exploring your own personal childhood experiences with death

My experience as a grief counselor has taught me that all too often care-givers-in-training want to rush into learning "techniques" to help children before they have even explored their own personal encounters with grief.

The purpose of this activity is to help you recall and explore your own early experiences with death. To help grieving kids, we as adults will find it invaluable to embrace our personal losses. In doing so, we can become more available to the children we want to help. In addition, we can remain conscious of not projecting our own "unfinished business" onto the children with whom we work.

This activity may help you determine your unwritten rules about death. I encourage you to discuss your responses with others. To explore your experiences with death, complete the following sentences. Be honest and thorough. Remember, there are no good or bad, right or wrong answers.

1. My first experience with death was....

2. Right after this first experience, I felt....

3. My primary source of emotional support during childhood was....

4. When death occurred in my family, my parents....

5. The biggest rule my family had about death was....

6. When I was a child, the worst thing about death was....

7. When I think about my childhood experiences with death, I realize....

8. As a child, these are the needs I had when someone (or something) close to me died....

9. Talking to children about death is....

10. When I think about children and funerals, I....

11. When people talk about children and death fifty years from now....

12. As a society, we teach children that death is....

We have all heard the statement, "If you want to help someone else, you've first got to help yourself." I hope that by completing the activity above, you will better understand how your own childhood experiences with death have influenced (and continue to influence) your life as well as your work with bereaved children.

To experience the death of a parent, grandparent, brother, sister, or best friend is among life's most stressful encounters for children. The specific roles the person who has died played in the child's life are critical to the child's self-definition. As ten-year-old Katie said after the death of her mother, "I used to have a mommy who loved me and took care of me. Now, I don't have a mommy here for me anymore." Obviously Katie was confronted with the difficult task of redefining herself without the presence of her loving mother.

As children work on this central need of mourning, every aspect of their capacity to cope is tested. The grieving child often finds herself thinking, feeling, and acting in ways that seem totally foreign. This process appears to be an inherent part of the search for a new identity in the absence of the person who died.

Social and functional role changes must be integrated into the bereaved child's new identity. For example, having a mother or father is typically a vital part of a child's self-concept. To go from having a mother or father to not having one is a process, not an event. Beyond the change in self-identity, there is also the loss of the "old" part of one's self—the significant part attached to one's parent. The child is mourning the loss not only on the outside, but on the inside.

The death of someone in the family also requires family members, children included, to take on new roles. For example, if Dad had always taken the garbage out and then he dies, someone still has to take out the garbage. If Mom always made breakfast and she dies, someone still has to make breakfast. The changed identity is confronted every time the child does something that the person who died used to do. Many outside observers are not aware of how difficult this can be for the child.

Well-intentioned yet misinformed adults sometimes reinforce a new "hyper-mature" identity on the part of the grieving child. This happens when comments such as this are made: "Now you have to be the man of the house." While everyone in the family will have new roles and responsibilities when a death occurs, we should never assign inappropriate role responsibilities to children. To encourage a boy or girl to be the "man" or "woman" of the house can damage his or her capacity to mourn and heal.

The trauma of grief for bereaved children can also result in what I would term a "regressive self-identity." Early on in grief there are often some regressive expressions of self-identity. You might observe the child teaching you that she has a temporary heightened dependence on others, feelings of helplessness, frustration, inadequacy, and fearfulness, as well as a generalized feeling of loss of control of her environment. These feelings usually hearken back to earlier developmental periods in which these self-images were a part of the child's learning experiences. These feelings can be frightening to the child, but they are actually a natural response to this reconciliation need of mourning.

During the early days of their grief journey, grieving children typically call on any and all of their resources just to survive. Their "regressive" thoughts, feelings and behaviors are a natural and appropriate means of trying to survive the trauma to their self-identity. As they begin to heal in grief, their need to regress typically lessens. If these regressive self-reflections do *not* change over time, the child is simply attempting to teach you about her need for support and understanding.

The bereaved child's identity is also impacted in that she becomes aware that she and others around her are mortal. She learns that she is not immune from the potential of experiencing losses in life. Some of these children develop a more serious or cautious view of themselves that reflects this sense of vulnerability. As caring adults, we must be watchful that this potential seriousness does not hinder the child's long-term capacity to play and have fun. Sometimes grieving children who haven't been helped to work through such feelings grow to become chronically depressed adults. This is a reminder that working with bereaved children is an excellent way of practicing preventive, proactive mental health care.

On the brighter side, I have also seen many bereaved children evolve more compassionate self-identities. They often develop a special sensitivity to the needs of others, demonstrate patience, and have a gift for being nurturing. Essentially, their experience of personal suffering can enhance their ability to be sensitive, compassionate, and aware of the needs of others who have losses in life. A way I like to say it is that the grieving child's gift in helping others often comes from embracing and learning from the pain of his own loss.

Each year thousands of bereaved children begin their encounter with this reconciliation need of mourning. Unfortunately, many of them will struggle with their changed identity alone and in isolation. We have a responsibility to companion grieving children as they struggle with many of these self-identity issues. Your desire to understand coupled with as much consistency, trust, and security in the child's environment as possible during this time are critically important!

Need 5. Relate the experience of the death to a context of meaning.

This reconciliation need involves allowing the child to search for and restore a sense of meaning in life after the death. After the death of someone loved, the child's perception of the meaning and purpose of life is naturally changed. Many adults are surprised to learn that even young children search for meaning when they are bereaved.

In the process of working on this reconciliation need of mourning, meaning is usually searched for through "How?" and "Why?" questions. The grieving child will only verbalize these to adults whom he trusts. When these conditions are met, the child will teach you about his search for meaning not only in words, but more frequently through play and acting-out behaviors.

A few examples of questions the child might naturally be exploring are: "How could a drunk driver crash and kill my Mommy?," "Why didn't my Daddy's body work right?," "How can my sister die when she is younger than me?"

It is interesting to note that many adults make the mistake of thinking they must always have answers to the bereaved child's cosmic questions. An essential component of truly helping grieving children is to know we don't have all the answers. In acknowledging our "not knowing," we ultimately become more helpful to the child who is searching for meaning. This may seem paradoxical, yet it appears to hold true in my work with thousands of bereaved children.

Inherent to the child's work on this reconciliation need is suffering. As caring adults, we naturally feel uncomfortable when we see a child who is hurting physically, emotionally, or spiritually. Yet, suffering is a painful yet natural part of the work of mourning.

So, perhaps it will be helpful to explore the role of suffering in the context of this central reconciliation need of childhood mourning. I do not mean to suggest that suffering is a naturally desirable event. However, suffering is as much a part of life as happiness is, and the way that we respond (regardless of chronological age) to unavoidable suffering will in many ways determine the meaning we give to life. Actually, we all in part heal through embracing hurt.

Our present western culture does not appear to understand the role of hurt, pain, and suffering in the healing process. We have to remind ourselves of the collective wisdom of the ages that says people reflect on the true meaning of life when they experience loss. Through the search for meaning many grieving kids have taught me that they have grown in ways that, without knowing the pain of human loss, they otherwise might not have grown.

I would be remiss here if I did not note that the many children subject to great hunger, poverty, and deprivation are not experiencing growth through such suffering. As a matter of fact, premature death is usually the consequence of this kind of suffering. This teaches us that basic security needs must be fulfilled before a bereaved child can do work related to the search for meaning.

However, when these basic needs are met, hundreds of grieving children have helped me understand that they can and do respond to the death with an amazing capacity to search for and find continued meaning in their lives:

- Six-year-old Charles taught me, "Ghosts have learned goodness from the people in my life who have died."

- Eight-year-old Diane taught me, "The people in Heaven have my grandma to watch over them now."

- Ten-year-old James taught me, "When I feel sad I think of all the fun times we had."

- Sixteen-year-old Shawn taught me, "Since my mom's death I'm very aware of other teenagers who I can help with their losses."

These are but a few examples of how children can and will teach you that if you allow them to ask "how" and "why" questions, they will search for—and find—continued meaning in life. If you disallow their mourning in general or project that you have all the answers, odds are that you will complicate this important task of mourning.

With support and understanding, bereaved children usually learn early in life that human beings cannot have complete control over themselves and their world. They learn that faith and hope are central to finding meaning in whatever one does in this short life. They learn a true appreciation for life and what it has to offer. They learn that it's the little things that sometimes matter the most. They learn a growing sense of gratefulness for all that life has to offer. They learn to look for the goodness in others. They learn an empathetic appreciation for the suffering of others. And, perhaps most of all, they learn how to meet not only their own needs, but how to help others meet theirs.

Need 6. Experience a continued supportive adult presence in future years.

We have come to understand that grief is a process, not an event. The long-term nature of grief means that grieving children will need adult "stabilizers" in their lives long after the event of the death. Unfortunately, because our society places so much value on the ability to "carry on," "keep your chin up," and, "keep busy," many bereaved children are abandoned shortly after the event of the death.

In spite of our awareness that children mourn long after the death occurs, attitudes are slow to change. "It will be best not to talk about it," "It's over and done with," and, "It's time to get on with life," still dominate the messages that many grieving kids are greeted with. Obviously, these kinds of messages inhibit grief rather than allow for its expression. Those who see children's grief as something that must be overcome or simply endured typically do not remain available to the child very long after the event of the death. In my observation, these adults encourage children to go around their grief instead of toward or through it.

Even those children who actively participate in the work of mourning will need stabilizing adults in their lives long after the event of the death. As the child grows into adulthood, she will mourn the loss in different ways at various developmental phases.

To be truly helpful, adult caregivers must appreciate the impact of loss on children. They must understand that to heal the child must be allowed and encouraged to mourn long after the event of the death. They must view grief not as an enemy to be overcome, but as a necessary consequence of having loved.

Stabilizing adults must also be aware that a child's griefbursts demand understanding, not judgment. Griefbursts often occur during pivotal life moments: birthdays (the child's or the deceased's); starting or getting out of school for the year; a change of seasons; receiving a report card; holidays; vacations; weekends; the child's first date; graduating from school; achieving a major goal; getting married; the birth of children; any kind of anniversary. These unsuspecting waves may come out of nowhere through a sight, a sound, or a smell. Unless the child (or adult who is reflecting on childhood loss) shares this experience with someone, he can and often does suffer in silence. As caring adults, we must stay alert for these griefbursts.

The "bereaved" label is an attempt on the part of society to identify a group of people with special needs. The grieving child does have special needs. One of the most important is the need to be companioned long after the event of the death. As we companion, we have a responsibility to remain available to these children long into the future.

*** *** ***

I hope this outline of reconciliation needs will assist you in companioning the bereaved children in your care. The responsibilities of adult caregivers are complex and ever-changing as the grieving child participates in the work of mourning. Helping the child meet these reconciliation needs demands your emotional and intellectual involvement. You must connect on not just a professional level, but a personal level as well. An authentic caregiver connects with the heart, not the head. Then and only then will the required safety occur for the child to "dose" herself on the six universal needs of mourning.

Chapter Five

Techniques for Counseling Grieving Children

The grief gardener's tools are the counseling techniques he calls upon as he companions the bereaved child. Just as the gardener learns to use different tools for different tasks—spades for digging, rakes for grading, hoes for weeding—the grief gardener uses different techniques as he helps each unique child meet the six reconciliation needs of mourning.

So the more tools the better, then? Yes and no. You must master the use of fundamental relationship skills before you pull any shiny new counseling techniques out of your toolshed. The grieving child will probably not be helped by the Tell-A-Story technique (p. 107), for example, if your attending and empathy skills are not razor sharp.

The next trick is knowing when and how to use a particular technique with a particular child. With experience and the supervision of mentor counselors, you will grow confident in the selection and use of bereavement counseling techniques.

What you will find in this chapter is a multitude of tools to choose from as you companion bereaved children. Pick and choose these selectively based on the needs of the child you are companioning. While it is beyond the scope of this text to **train** you in the use of each technique, I do recommend *The Companioning the Grieving Child Curriculum Book: Activities to Help Children and Teens Heal* by Patricia Morrissey, available through my bookstore at centerforloss.com. This book will help you further understand activities mentioned here. It also offers a plethora of other activities that will provide you with more insight and training in companioning children through grief.

The following categories of counseling techniques are described in this chapter: play therapy, art therapy, "word" therapy, music therapy, and a catch-all category I've called "potpourri." Under each of these broad headings are therapeutic rationales and, in many cases, a number of specific techniques that you can try straight off the page.

Play Therapy

I believe that play is the grieving child's natural method of self-expression and communication. Play allows the child to embody the "teach me" principle that is the theme of this text. Children often use play in response to losses because they are trying to learn about what no one can teach them. It is through their play that they have taught me about the meaning of death in their lives. For bereaved children, "playing out" their grief thoughts and feelings is a natural and self-healing process.

Play is a child's natural method of self-expression and communication. It helps children relate to the world around them and gives them the freedom to explore and express their feelings when they may be developmentally unable to do so verbally. When a child's world is impacted by death, his pain and loss are often expressed through the use of play. A very wise person once said, "Play is the child's response to life." That includes a child's response to death.

Play: misunderstood and minimized

To deny play to a grieving child is to deny her the right to mourn and heal. How can a hurting child feel that it's OK to play when he hears messages like, "You need to take care of your Mom now," or, "Be the big man of the house now." These kinds of messages emphasize that this is no time for play, but instead a time for a child to be serious.

Why is it that our culture generally doesn't value play as a natural right and feels people must "earn it" after the work gets done? Play can be, in fact, very **productive** in helping children process unexpressed feelings of grief. Play is especially helpful in providing children a way to bring their feelings out safely and at their own pace.

As Americans, we sometimes have a need to be serious. To "be serious" and "to play" are often seen as opposites. Children are taught to be serious about behaving properly, performing in school and getting into the right college. To "be serious" implies in our culture that there is a "right" way and a "wrong" way to do things, and that we should make no mistakes along the way. If we are not "serious" about it, we might not do it "right."

Many children are not taught the **emotional** skills they need to survive the universal experiences of life, love, and loss. Play encourages development of the emotional skills that children need as they grow to adulthood. Play provides a safe and creative place to express their innermost feelings.

Play therapy: my philosophy

Prior to entering the playroom, counselors who work with bereaved children should know **why** they will do what they're about to do. In other words, counselors must already have in hand their own personal theory of the ways in which play therapy works (and doesn't work). Theory helps create a framework for how the counselor works to help grieving children.

Without asking the following questions, a counselor who works with bereaved children is not likely to continue to grow as a helper: What is happening here? Why am I using play to assist this grieving child in the healing process? What are my assumptions about the child's need to mourn? What accounts for the observations I am making? Asking yourself these questions encourages you to articulate your assumptions about counseling bereaved children and can also help you generate new ideas about how to be helpful.

In an attempt to encourage you to write down your own thoughts about grieving kids and play, I will express my own set of guiding principles. The following observations are reasons I believe play therapy to be invaluable in helping bereaved children do the work of mourning:

1. *Play is the child's natural method of self-expression and communication.*

2. *Play permits and encourages the child to express difficult, painful emotions in ways she can't verbally.*

3. *Play is often the child's natural response to the death of someone loved.*

4. *Play is an essential ingredient in establishing a therapeutic relationship with a grieving child.*

5. *Play assists the counselor in understanding the inner world of the bereaved child.*

6. *Play increases the child's involvement and interest in the helping process.*

7. *Play allows for the use of fantasy.*

8. *Play allows the child to teach the counselor.*

9. *Play is energizing and refreshing.*

10. *Play is a loving, compassionate way to help grieving children heal.*

Play affirms life

Play, for a child in pain, is necessary to affirm that life will continue in the absence of someone loved. Turning to play as he confronts the death allows the child to confirm his own continued living. Play provides a place to transcend ordinary levels of being and experience an inner world of peace, love, and safety.

A naive counselor may ask a young bereaved child, "What brings you here today?" A shrug of the shoulder or a blank stare would be the likely response. Few children in our mourning-avoiding culture will talk about struggling with their grief, even when adults around them see their calls for help, such as regressive and acting-out behaviors. Fortunately, the tools of play therapy can be used to create an environment where the counselor can compassionately accompany the child on his journey into grief.

As Arnold Gessall, a leading child development specialist, has written, "Children reveal themselves most transparently in their play life."

Play Techniques

Here are a few of the types of play I've used successfully with grieving children:

Physical self-expression

A child with internalized grief often wants to engage in physical activities. Because protest (explosive emotions) is often part of the child's grief journey, have available means to allow for its expression. Get creative; offer punching bags, boxing gloves, soccer balls, footballs, basketballs. You can also help the child know that when she feels things are all bottled up, there are appropriate ways to express herself—running around the house ten times, hitting the punching bag—whatever works for her. This helps the child make a connection between her feelings and actions.

Voice recorders and play telephones

Some kids don't want to write in a journal but will keep a talking journal. Kids can record thoughts and feelings as they come up at home.

Play telephones (or walkie-talkies) encourage the child to chat with you about whatever he wants to. I invite children to go into a separate room as we talk on the phone. The distance sometimes helps them feel safe.

Stuffed animals

My Center is full of stuffed animals. Have you ever noticed there is a sense of safety and comfort they provide? Just having them present is a counseling technique in and of itself. I invite children to pick one out to watch over for me. They are usually happy to tell me what they did with the animal at home.

Puppets

Puppets offer a certain anonymity and distance that often frees the bereaved child. Have a big box of several different characters available. Encourage play. Talk to the puppet and ask how it feels, engage the puppet with your own puppet, create a puppet show with a story theme, or even make puppets with the child.

Dollhouses

Wow! I've learned a lot from kids playing with a dollhouse. They will often assign roles to the different dolls and play out home scenes that are rich with meaning.

The Jeep technique

When I need a special, safe yet fun place for grieving kids to share their thoughts and feelings with me, I take them out to my Jeep. The child sits in the driver's seat (which puts him in control) and I sit in the back (which means he doesn't have to look directly at me), and we pretend to go on a picnic. We "go" wherever the child drives us. But during our journey, the child often spontaneously expresses thoughts and feelings about the death as well. The pretend trip seems to create enough distance from the pain of the grief that the child feels safe to approach that pain.

Art Therapy

Art therapy provides a natural avenue for children to express their thoughts and feelings. I have learned so much from bereaved children by simply having colored pencils, crayons, felt-tipped markers, and lots of paper available.

I'll never forget the three-year-old boy who picked up a pencil and paper from my floor and spontaneously drew a mommy whale, a daddy whale, and a baby whale. (His father had recently died in an airplane crash.) He said (pointing to his picture), "The whales are a family. Do I still have a family?"

Art in grief counseling with children is beneficial in some of the following ways: 1) art allows for expression of explosive emotions, sadness, and pain that a child might hesitate to talk about; 2) while doing art, the child is in control, which gives him a sense of self-control; 3) art provides counselors access to unconscious thoughts and feelings.

Selecting art materials

The grieving child will often gravitate toward the medium that he is comfortable expressing himself through. Offer several different art tools and materials: paint, crayons, chalk, markers, glue, buttons, paper, cloth, felt, clay, etc.

Drawing

Free drawing is very helpful in having bereaved children teach me about their unique grief journeys. There is freedom in drawing whatever you want. Give verbal support at appropriate times.

Five-year-old Charles, whose little brother died from heart disease, drew a house. He told a story about the house and a boy who lived there. Then he drew the little boy trying to lift the house up off the ground. Grieving kids have taught me through their art how they often try to compensate for their feelings of helplessness.

Five faces technique

Have the child draw faces depicting various feelings, such as sadness, anger and happiness. From the interaction that evolves, the child teaches you about her feelings.

Free painting

Painting is another excellent avenue for working with bereaved children. As the paint flows, feelings often get expressed, directly and indirectly.

Painting is particularly useful with preschool through second grade children. I often encourage free painting but sometimes I suggest a child paints what she is feeling right now.

I once asked seven-year-old Jason, whose grandparents had been killed in a drunk-driving car crash, how he felt when he was sad. He painted a little black ball and later said, "I feel really little when I am sad." I didn't interpret but just expressed interest and let him stay in the teacher role.

The very act of painting or drawing, with no counselor involvement, helps the child with self-esteem and expression of feelings. From this as a starting place, a variety of options evolve:

- Invite the child to describe the picture as if it were the child, i.e. "Pretend you are the dinosaur and help me learn about you."

- Invite the child to tell a story about the drawing or painting.

- Watch for changes in his body posture, facial expression, tone of voice, and use of silence.

Clay

Clay encourages expression of thoughts and feelings. I like it because it's messy! It appeals across age groups. Clay can be formed into a variety of shapes, pounded, cut, and thrown. When I use clay with a grieving child, I spread lots of newspaper out on the floor, then I have small pans of water available to help in molding and smoothing. Use a pencil for poking, and a rubber mallet for shaping. You should get involved, too. It's an excellent relationship builder.

Jim, age eight, whose brother died from a brain tumor, used clay to mold the doctor who took care of his little brother. He then used a pencil to poke holes in this effigy. Obviously, he was using clay to express anger at the doctor.

Collages of feelings

Collages of different words and pictures from magazines help kids portray a variety of feelings. Invite the child to pick and choose different feelings that they have had or are now experiencing and paste them on poster board.

Photography

My favorite use of photography with bereaved children is as follows: The child has a camera and I have a camera. We invite each other to take pictures of anything at first. Then I say, "How about if we make some faces of different feelings. Can you make a face like when you are happy, sad, mad, etc.?" We take turns shooting each other's faces. We look at the photos on my computer or we print them out, put them on the wall, and talk about them.

I always invite kids to bring in photos of the person in their life who has died. I learn more in a few minutes of photo sharing than I might in a day of just talking.

Music Therapy

The therapeutic value of musical expression has long been known in almost every culture in the world. I keep a guitar in my office. I'm amazed how kids are drawn to it and often want to strum on it. I've often had kids invite me to teach them a few chords on the guitar. This may evolve into wanting to make up songs.

Many children enjoy using rhythm, like tambourines, bells, and drums. I might say: "Show me what kind of drum beat you would use to show you are sad, happy, mad, etc.?" I've found music to be a great relationship-builder.

Word Therapy

Word therapy includes anything that has to do with words: writing, reading, storytelling, and talking. Below are several forms of "word" therapy.

Journals

A feeling journal is a tablet in which a child is encouraged to record her thoughts and feelings during her grief journey. The journal is just for her and is only shared with the counselor or others if the child chooses to. This works well with quiet, introspective children.

Letters

Letters to the person who died or to oneself can be invaluable in having the child teach you about thoughts and feelings. Writing the letter is a form of mourning, because the child takes what is on the inside and expresses it on the outside. I have found it particularly useful to invite children to write a letter to themselves.

Poetry

Poetry often comes from deep in the hearts of the children. Poetry frees them to express what they really, truly feel. You can often inspire the child to come up with a poem by modeling one of your own bad poems. You can then laugh together and learn together.

Essays

Essays are more for grieving teens than for younger children. If the child has had a decent relationship with the person who died, I often suggest the following: "How about writing an essay, a story that you title 'A Tribute to (Name of Person Who Died)'?" This is very open-ended and allows the teen to go wherever he wants with it.

Books

Carefully selected books, specific to the unique needs of a particular child, can help children with a variety of life difficulties. Because loss is a part of all phases of life, it is natural that loss is a common theme in books for both children and adults. Today you can find a plethora of books on death, dying, and grief. A number of death-related bibliographies have even become available.

In my experience with thousands of bereaved children, written words are less intrusive and demanding than spoken words. As with play, art, and music, children approach books with a minimum of defensive posturing.

Tell-a-Story technique

Invite the child to create a story with you. The story becomes a metaphor for aspects of the child's real-life experiences. Start with an opening line, letting them fill in the next part. For example, I say, "Once there was a girl who liked to...." The child then may say "play." I proceed with a series of questions related to her answer, such as: What did she like to play? Who did she play with? What was her friend's name? As I continue to ask questions and the story builds, I present a problem, like a character getting mad, and then I lead up to a solution, such as "One day a fairy came to her and said, "If you say what you really want, it will come true. What did she say she wanted?"

The hope is that the child will present a problem she is feeling and come up with a solution that will bring some peace. In the end I ask how she would like the story to end, and if the character is like her and if so, in what way. This technique gives you an idea of how the child is processing her loss, and an idea of her fears and hopes.

The Jimmy Green technique

I have had success in drawing grieving kids out with the Jimmy Green technique. This is when you as counselor describe the child's fears as being similar to the fears of a hypothetical child, whom I call Jimmy Green. In doing this you indirectly give the child permission to feel feelings and to recognize the naturalness of these feelings.

For example, I might say, "You know, Zach, I knew a boy not very long ago who had a fear a lot like yours. His name was Jimmy Green. His dad died too and he really got scared about going to school. Sometimes he would get a stomachache and would tell his mom, and she really didn't know what to do. Well, after Jimmy and I talked for a while, we got an idea about what was bothering him. He was afraid that if he went to school and left his mom alone that something might happen to her. He was so scared that he thought he better just stay at home with his mom. You know, Zach, it sounds like you might have some feelings like Jimmy Green did. Jimmy and I talked about his feelings when we met together, and after a while it wasn't so scary for him to go to school. Do you think maybe you and I could talk like Jimmy and I did?"

Sentence completion inventories

One of the most valuable techniques I have ever used with bereaved children is sentence completion inventories. This is simply where you provide the beginning of sentences and then invite the child to complete them. This can be done out loud with the child or she can write down her responses.

Pick and choose appropriate lead-ins for the sentences given the unique situation. An example of a sentence completion inventory follows:

1. Sometimes I wish that….

2. If I could only….

3. Sometimes I pretend that….

4. I can't understand….

5. My friends are….

6. I get mad when….

7. Since my (Dad) died, I….

8. I worry that….

9. I'm happy when….

10. At home things are….

Wishes and fears inventory

Ask the child to teach you about some wishes and fears. I often say, "If you could have two or three wishes, what would they be? If you have two or three fears, what might those be?" Sometimes you can learn a lot.

Five feelings technique

While children will often teach you more through their behaviors than through their words, the five feelings technique sometimes works. This is where you attempt to make talking about feelings easier for the grieving child by asking, "Did you know there are five common feelings that both adults and children have: sad, glad, mad, scared, and lonely? Let's see if you ever have any of these feelings. Since your Dad died, have you had some sad feelings?" Some children like to respond nonverbally by spreading their hands apart relating how much, if any, they have experienced or are experiencing these particular feelings.

Potpourri

Below are a number of other techniques that I have found helpful while companioning children through grief.

Nature

Talk counseling alone with bereaved children does not help them reconcile death loss into their young lives. Yet something even simpler does: experiencing nature. The great outdoors is a naturally healing place. The more kids learn to simply experience a love of nature and times of quiet reflection in nature, the more they learn about themselves and about life and death.

I remember seeing five-year-old Jamie for her third counseling session. Her 42-year-old father recently died of a sudden heart attack. Jamie is naturally shy, and I could sense that she internally questioned if she could trust me to share her deep feelings. Spontaneously we left my office and walked outside atop the mountain foothills where the Center for Loss sits. We ambled down a boardwalk that leads to a gazebo set among a stand of beautiful pines. As we approached the gazebo, a mule deer fawn suddenly captured our attention. Jamie stopped. Her face lit up with awe. In the midst of her sadness, she experienced a moment of joy, thanks to Mother Earth.

5 Tips for Exploring Nature with Children

1. **Teach less, explore more.** Share your own awe of nature. I share my respect for the way a cactus can survive and thrive in such dry conditions. Sharing my own sense of wonder encourages the child to do so, too. An amazing trust and helping alliance between adult and child also naturally evolves.

2. **Be spontaneous and receptive.** The outdoors creates a spontaneous excitement in the child that can be naturally therapeutic. Nature teaches us to be aware and open to experience. Keep in mind that every question, every comment is an opportunity to communicate with the child. Nature provides many metaphors about life and death.

3. **Experience first, talk later.** Children have a natural gift for embracing the moment they are experiencing. Allow them to experience the moment; talk, if it comes at all, can come later.

4. **Provide praise and patience.** Show interest in their discoveries and reactions. This feeds their energy and self-esteem. Nature has a way of inviting children in, but don't try to rush the child.

5. **Be playful and joyful.** Children are naturally drawn to nature if you keep the experience fun and relaxing.

Candle ritual

This technique can be used to help children see and understand that their love for someone goes on even after a death. In fact, many kids, directly or indirectly, will teach you that this is often a question they have within.

To enact the candle ritual, you hold one candle and say, "When you were born you had a gift to give love and receive love. This gift is like a light; it makes you feel warm and happy."

Then you light the candle that represents the child, and say, "At first you got close to your mom. She probably held you and fed you. You felt very close to her."

Then you take an unlit candle, place it next to the unlit candle representing the mother, and touch them together so it lights.

"Your Dad also loved you very much. He played with you, he held you, he smiled at you, he played games with you. You felt close to him (put the child's candle next to a candle representing the father until it lights) and you lit a love light with him too."

"Last year your Dad had a heart attack and he died. The warm, loving part of him was gone. But you have kept on loving him even though he is dead, and your light has stayed burning. You don't have to blow out your love light that is lit for him. You will always have memories of your Dad and be able to remember the love he had for you."

Pause from time to time. Children sometimes have questions or want to add to the story.

Don't end quickly. Explain that even though we will now blow out the candles (invite the child to blow out the candles when she is ready), the love the child has for her dad will go on and on.

Memory ritual

I often use this technique with the child's entire family or significant others. This is where you place two or three large candles in the middle of a table. Around the outside of the table are small candles (one in front of each person). The purpose of this ritual is to assist in memory work: sharing memories of the person who died.

Begin with this: "We come together tonight to remember someone you all loved. Let's start by listening to a piece of music that your mom liked very much. (Or a reading, or both.)

Next, invite the person to your left to share a memory, and so on until everyone who wants to, shares. People find this to be a powerfully healing ritual.

Memory books and boxes

Memory books and memory boxes are naturals in assisting the grieving child in doing memory work. **Memory books** can be as creative as the child wants them to be. Collect a series of photographs of the dead person's life and put them in a photo album. Underneath the photos the child can write down memories. Let them decorate and write as much as they wish. If kids are reluctant, show an example to stimulate interest.

A **memory box** is a place for bereaved children to store keepsakes of the person who died. Using a shoebox or other cardboard box, have the child decorate the outside and then fill it with photos, keepsakes, poems, rocks, shells—whatever will help the child remember the person who died and memorialize his unique relationship with that person.

Remember that companioning is an art, and techniques should never be viewed as recipes to resolve a child's grief. Regardless of what combination of techniques is used, when we companion, we stay attuned to the always-evolving process with the unique child. As trust builds, grieving kids will teach us what techniques help them heal.

✳ ✳ ✳

In the next chapter we'll explore the family systems approach to counseling grieving children. Involving the family is vital in helping kids heal.

Chapter Six

A Family Systems Approach to Companioning the Grieving Child

For better or worse, we as grief companions do not control the grieving child's environment. We see a bereaved child one, two, **maybe** three hours a week. The child spends his remaining 165 hours a week with his parents, his siblings, his classmates, his friends. All these people influence his mourning; they form his day-to-day environment.

The traditional mental health understanding of grief has, like our culture in general, tended to forget this. Many counselors have been trained to believe that grief is a private, individual crisis. Yet I believe that a family systems approach is the most appropriate one in helping us understand both children's and adults' response to death. In developing my theory of family-oriented bereavement counseling, I hope to inspire you to consider its relevance whether you are working with an individual child and using a family **orientation**, or working with the entire family as a unit of care.

To understand a particular grieving child's needs, we must understand the systems in which the bereaved child operates: the culture, the community, the classroom, and most importantly, the family. The caregiver who receives training in a family perspective sees human beings as "belonging to something." The "thing" to which they belong is invariably a larger group of people—a family. Sometimes it is a Ward and June Cleaver-style nuclear family, sometimes it is a nontraditional family, and sometimes for children it is a temporary foster family. But regardless of the family make-up, a grieving child cannot be considered as separate from the social context in which he or she lives.

The family is the primary space in which the child learns through day-to-day living. The quality of the family environment (and rules surrounding death, grief, and mourning) is a major influence on the bereaved child's capacity to mourn in healthy ways.

Why many of us don't "do" family systems counseling

Despite the best intentions and sound ideological convictions, bereavement counselors' delivery of family-oriented care (across age-groups) is still quite limited in reality. The reasons for this gap are varied and complex, but one of the needs is for a practical, understandable conceptual framework for understanding the counselor's role with the family.

My observation suggests that many grief counselors, often through no fault of their own, have received little if any training in family systems approaches to counseling. Terms like "family adaptability," "family homeostasis," and "structural family therapy" may overwhelm the grief counselor who is brave enough to wander into the family counseling literature. While these concepts may be important to understanding family systems theory, they are not always useful in helping the counselor make practical decisions about helping the grieving child and family. In actuality, many of the helping approaches developed for family counseling come from specialists in family therapy—who often don't have extensive experience in companioning bereaved children. It seems we might have something to learn from each other.

In addition, most grief counselors are appropriately reluctant to make use of powerful family counseling techniques without special training. The result is that the family systems perspective tends to be talked about more in theory than applied in actual grief counseling. My hope in this chapter is to help try to begin to bridge this gap.

The illusion of the dyad in child bereavement counseling

If family systems concepts have not been well integrated into grief counseling practices, part of the reason is that the family has been perceived as separate from the counselor's involvement in the system. The counselor has often been taught to be an observer of the family system rather than a participant in the family system. As leading family therapists such as Haley, Minuchin, and Satir have historically emphasized, the central unit in family counseling is not the family alone, but the therapeutic system, which includes both the family and the counselor. Therefore, a logical starting point for a model of the counselor's role in helping grieving families, then, is that the counselor is part of the system.

A view of the counseling relationship between the counselor and bereaved child can be referred to as "the illusion of the dyad in grief counseling." Why? Because, even when they are not physically present in counseling sessions, family members are very much involved in what goes on between the counselor and the grieving child.

Family members (or guardians with whom bereaved children reside) influence, if not outright decide on, the selection of the counselor and expectations the child has of the counseling process. Most also carry out suggested helping principles to assist the grieving child. Essentially, the family has the "ghost of presence" even when they are not a part of the counseling interaction. Therefore, every counselor who companions bereaved children is involved in a therapeutic triad of counselor-child-family. It's time to acknowledge the ghost!

There can be no doubt that the counselor-grieving child relationship is multilateral as opposed to bilateral. While most counselor-child interactions take place on a one-to-one basis, the therapeutic **environment** includes not only the child's family, but other influences such as peers, school, media, and society in general.

You will note that the center of the therapeutic environment is formed by the child, the child's family, and the counselor. I will call this the therapeutic triad. Of all the relationships in this triangle, the counselor-child relationship has been given the most focused attention in the bereavement literature. Additional perspectives on the therapeutic triad are introduced below.

- *The family's support of the child*

   While counselors usually companion children in their own offices, the helping strategies proposed by the counselor are typically carried out at home in the family environment. Consequently, counselors who fail to perceive and make use of the helping role of the family are failing to make use of a systems model of caregiving.

   The family's involvement in and commitment to helping the bereaved child is critical to the child's healing. Outside the counseling office, the counselor has little influence over the implementing of proposed helping strategies. My experience suggests that the family generally has the greatest influence.

   Does this mean you that you can't help a grieving child except within the four walls of your office? No! But it does mean that to best help the child, you must mobilize the collaborative efforts of the therapeutic triad (as well as other influential elements in the therapeutic environment).

- *The counselor-grieving child relationship*

  While we need more formal studies, my experience suggests that the quality of the counselor's relationship with the bereaved child's family may determine the quality of the relationship that develops between the counselor and child. It only makes sense that counselors who relate well to the child but not to adult family members (if they relate at all) will end up with less collaborative helping assistance from the family.

  Without family assistance, working effectively with the grieving child may be impossible. Generally, one would anticipate that the more complicated the bereavement circumstances (nature of the death, level and nature of attachment of the child to the deceased, etc.), the more important the counselor-family relationship would become.

- *The counselor's support of the grieving child-family relationship*

  In exploring important concepts of human development a number of years ago, Vrie Brofensbrenner suggested that the quality of primary dyadic relationships (such as husband-wife or parent-child) is influenced by the support given those relationships by significant outsiders. For example, marital relationships are strengthened or weakened by the influence of in-laws; the mother-child relationship depends on the support of the father.

  As a significant outsider in family relationships, the counselor invariably has an effect—positive or negative. For example, in supporting the family in coping with the death of one of its members, the counselor may be able to help maintain open, healthy patterns of communication during this naturally stressful period. However, if the counselor over-engages with the bereaved child (perhaps even in a codependent way) to the exclusion of the family, then the counselor is unknowingly undermining the family's internal relationships. The irony is that the most positive relationship between the counselor and the grieving child may serve to weaken family relationships ***if the counselor is oblivious to the fact that she is involved in a therapeutic triad***.

- *The family's support of the counselor-grieving child relationship*

  The family has the potential to either support or undermine the counselor's relationship with the bereaved child. In an effort to protect the interests of their child, the family is constantly assessing the perceived skill level and caring concern of the counselor. If a child resists going to a counseling session, if a helping strategy suggested by the counselor doesn't seem to actually help, or if a counselor cancels a scheduled appointment or is generally unavailable, the family may grow to distrust the counselor.

The model of the therapeutic triad suggests that a vital element in the continuation of a supportive counselor-grieving child relationship will be the family's support of the counselor's role. The following are examples of family responses that support the counselor-grieving child relationship:

- "Dr. Wolfelt really seems to want to help you."

- "Why don't you tell Dr. Wolfelt about all those mixed-up feelings you've been having?"

On the other hand, here are some undermining responses:

- "He probably doesn't know what he's going to do with you."

- "All he does is play with you."

Family Systems Caregiving Strategies

The traditional approach to caregiving with bereaved children has been to focus on the individual child without much involvement (if any) from the family. I am proposing that counseling of the grieving child should be carried out with direct family involvement when possible. I advocate "family-oriented bereavement counseling." The key difference between a counselor who thinks in family systems terms and one who practices a family systems approach is that the latter regularly integrates the family into the counseling process.

This is not to suggest that the entire family must be present for all counseling sessions. On the contrary, I generally have an initial family session early on in the counseling process and then move the family in and out of sessions depending on the unique needs that evolve over time.

When and which family members to invite depends on the unique needs of each situation. Bringing together the relevant "family" may at times mean inviting the bereaved child's teacher, clergyperson, grandparent, or neighbor. The key is to think creatively about the multifaceted influences on the grieving child's journey into grief.

When the family is directly involved in the etiology of the bereaved child's need for counseling (e.g. when mom has died and dad remarries a neighbor four months later and says to the child, "This is your new Mother; don't talk about your old Mother."), then the family's communication pattern may constitute the primary focus of counseling efforts.

The roles and goals of the family-oriented grief companion

- *Create a safe place for mourning*

  Perhaps the family counselor's most important role is creator of a safe mourning environment for grieving children and their families. You might think of your counseling office as a greenhouse—a sheltered, warm, nurturing place in which fragile seedlings can go about growing and maturing without the distractions and detractions of everyday life.

  The materials with which you build this greenhouse are the concepts in this book. The family grief gardener uses self, group process, and knowledge of family systems to facilitate the six needs of mourning and to help integrate the death into the life of the child and the family. She is a participant-observer—open, honest, and direct. She supports growth while embracing the pain of the death and the ripple effect of losses the death initiates.

  In sum, this role involves providing security at a natural time of insecurity, emotional and spiritual support at a time when this may be lacking, and understanding and acceptance when it may not exist elsewhere.

✳ ✳ ✳ ✳ ✳ ✳ ✳ ✳ ✳

Individual, family, or support group counseling?

Counselors often ask me when they should see the child individually, when they should see the child with his family, and when they should refer the child to a support group.

There may be times when you use one or all three of these helping avenues. Even when I'm seeing a child individually, I'm always seeing their world from a family systems perspective. My own preference is to do some work with the child individually (which helps relieves pressure from the "pressure cooker" grief can cause in a family) while integrating the family into sessions from time to time.

✳ ✳ ✳ ✳ ✳ ✳ ✳ ✳ ✳

- *Help the family understand grief*

  Find appropriate ways and times to teach bereaved families about grief and the effects it may have on their family system. For example, while children and adults share similar emotions of grief, children are likely to respond with an apparent "lack of feelings." Adults often need help in understanding the normalcy of the child's seemingly capricious shifts from acute sadness to apparent indifference and back again.

  The family may also need help in understanding that the grieving child will mourn in doses as she grows older and views her grief anew from different developmental standpoints. Likewise, many adults need help in understanding that people do not "get over" grief and that while children do not forget their grief, they do not keep it constantly in front of them, either.

  Another common grief response families need help in understanding is the "pressure-cooker" phenomenon. When death impacts a family, everyone has a high need to feel understood yet a natural incapacity to be understanding. Knowing this often happens lessens adult feelings of guilt about not being as available to the child as they might like to be. Learning about the pressure cooker phenomenon can also free the adults in the family system to do their own work of mourning so they can eventually focus more on the child.

  These are but a few of many teachings the family counselor might share with bereaved families. Take your own "teacher" cues from the unique needs of the families in your care.

- *Offer an outside perspective*

  Closely aligned with the teacher role is that of helping the family see more clearly what is happening in their individual and family life. The counselor can help by describing or reflecting back to the family observations on the impact of the death on the family. Really, the counselor is providing the family with "new lenses," since the family often may be viewing their situation through tunnel vision. In other words, the companion brings objectivity and a sense of normalcy to the family.

- *Help adults understand the grieving child's behavior*

  When a flower wilts, it is telling us it needs water. When its leaves turn yellow, it may be telling us it is getting too much water. When a grieving child behaves in certain ways, she is telling us something, too.

Part of your job is to help other adults in the child's life, especially parents, understand the needs that underlie behaviors. For example, an angry, acting-out child feels helpless and in "misbehaving," is expressing her feelings of insecurity. If you can reframe such behaviors for adults, you are helping them to become more supportive and understanding of the child's attempts to alert the family system to her pain.

- *Point out discrepancies in communication within the family*

  During a family session, a bereaved child's father says to you, "Sam's doing great!" Yet, Sam's extensive acting-out tells you that this is not the case. When discrepancies such as this become apparent to you, it is your role to point them out to the family. For example, you might, after talking with the family, intuit that they have this common, unspoken rule: "Death isn't something we talk about." Yet some members of the family will likely exhibit a need to talk about it. You can help by articulating the unspoken rule and gently bringing the family around to discussing the rule's origin.

- *Help delineate changed roles within the family*

  Counselors help all members of the family sort out changed roles. If Mom died and she usually washed the dishes, someone still has to wash the dishes. You can help families talk such role changes through. At the same time, you must also help guard against inappropriate role assignments within the family. A 12-year-old cannot and should not be expected to assume a parental role in the family, for example. In other words, you can help counter expectations (stated or unstated) that a child can somehow replace the dead person within the family.

- *Build self-esteem*

  The family grief companion helps build the self-esteem of all family members. When I observe parents with their grieving daughter, I might say to them, "I see how Emma feels cared about and safe with you." Reminders such as these help them feel appreciated as caregivers—something they need during this difficult time.

  I have found that play is the best way to build the self-esteem of bereaved children. When I allow them to enjoy the moment, they feel good about themselves.

- *Reconstruct the family's loss history*

  The family grief companion not only assists in mourning the present death, but also stays sensitive to the overall family loss history. You can help grieving families understand that they may not only be mourning this loss, but prior losses as well. Genograms (a format for drawing a family tree that records information about family members and their relationships over at least three generations) can be a helpful tool in understanding the family's loss history.

- *Facilitate ritual as a means of healing*

  While companioning, explore with the bereaved family how or if they have used ritual to assist both the children and adults in the healing process. Help the family understand the need to involve children in ritual. Stepping into your teacher role again, make them aware that when words are inadequate, ceremony can assist in the healing process.

  One important reminder here: It is never too late to make use of ritual. Families who may have missed the healing benefits of a meaningful funeral ceremony can still be helped by mourning rituals today and into the future. Help them plan a memorial ceremony (even if the death happened some time ago), make a memory table, plant a tree, carry out the candle ritual described in this book—any ritual that will help them acknowledge the reality of their loss and begin to meet the other reconciliation needs of mourning.

- *Act as family advocate*

  The counselor may be placed in the position of suggesting what is in the best interests of the child and family. I was called in to testify in court regarding the needs of one family's children when the mother shot and killed her husband. Rather than sending the children to separate foster homes (which the court was about to do), I said they should be brought back together under the care of someone they already knew and trusted before the tragedy.

  In another family advocate situation, I brought a church leader into a counseling session to supportively confront his belief (which was severely complicating the child's and the family's mourning) that mourning and faith are mutually exclusive.

  One final, practical way to act as family advocate in times of grief is to write a note to school administrators and even corporate human

✻ ✻

The Grieving Family

Ten Realities

1. Traditional mental health care assumptions about grief have generally reflected those of the broader culture.

2. The death of a family member results in special needs for the family as a unit. The death of any member results in reorganization of the system.

3. A bereaved child's grief journey is particularly vulnerable to the help or lack of help provided by significant adults in the child's life.

4. Children can cope with what they know. They cannot cope with what they don't know. When significant adults give incomplete or false information, they hinder the child's ability to cope.

5. Children mourn not just the death, but the changes that death brings about in their world.

6. Family rules about death teach children what death should mean to them. An open family system acknowledges feelings, while a closed family system denies feelings about death.

7. Grief and ways of mourning can be handed down generation to generation.

8. New phases of family development result in new acknowledgments of the death and a reworking of the six central needs of mourning.

9. The counselor who wants to supportively companion grieving children and families must be aware of her own family system grief issues.

10. The bereaved child's and family's response to the death must be respected as the family's best response given the backdrop of family history.

✻ ✻

resource executives requesting additional "bereavement leave" after a death. The traditional 72 hours off is not nearly enough for children and adults alike to return to school and work.

- *Validate all family members for the courage to mourn*

  The family grief companion provides support and encouragement for all family members to mourn. While he brings objectivity to the helping process, he also sees himself as a humble guide, a caring companion, and a privileged witness to the healing process. See strengths, bring hope, and encourage healing!

- *Provide hope for healing*

  When a child is referred for counseling, it is not unusual that the entire family system is pervaded by a depressive mood. Obviously, bereavement brings with it sadness and depression. A vital role is to nourish hope for not only the child's capacity to heal, but for the entire family's capacity to heal.

  The importance of this role cannot be overstated; without hope, healing cannot and will not occur. All members of the family garden may have been assaulted by a hailstorm, yet the family grief gardener looks for strengths in the child's and the family's underlying roots and points out these strengths at appropriate times: "You made some important decisions that resulted in a meaningful funeral for your family."

  Basically, build on individual and family self-esteem, all the while understanding the role of self-esteem in the eventual reconciliation process. In effect, say to the child and family, "See what healing decisions you have already made. See how far you have come. You are making progress and I believe you have the inner strength to survive and to be happy again."

✳ ✳ ✳

It's obvious that children need support within the family when someone they love has died. By supporting the family, we support the child. Yet children also need support outside their family systems—in particular, at school. The next chapter discusses how we, as counselors, can support children as they navigate their way through their school days.

Chapter Seven

Helping Grieving Children at School

Schools are the child's primary environment during the school year. So, especially in a society looking more and more to its schools as a provider of not just education but also social and emotional guidance, schools are an important source of support for grieving kids. Teachers, especially, are very important to their students. From them they learn not only facts and figures, but also behaviors and emotions. Kids rely on teachers for support during the seven or so hours they are in school each day. In many ways, teachers and counselors are not just imparters of knowledge to children, but they are also authority figures, role models, friends, and confidants during the school day.

School isn't just a place for book learning. It's a home away from home, a place for students to share their lives with others. When a student is grieving, he needs to share his new and scary feelings. He needs to know that like home (we hope), school will be a stable and loving refuge.

Talking to children about death

If you are a teacher or counselor, you are probably good at talking to children. You know that they respond better, for example, when you get down on their level and maintain eye contact. You ask open-ended questions to solicit their thoughts and feelings. Without talking down to them, you use language that they understand. Keep up the good work. You'll need all these skills as you help students grieve. But you may find that talking about death isn't so easy. That's OK. Our culture as a whole has a hard time discussing death. Actually, what grieving children need most is for someone to listen to and understand them—not to talk at them. Instead of worrying about what to say, try to create opportunities for your grieving student to talk to *you* about the death.

Learn about grief

To help your students cope with death and grief, you must continually enhance your own knowledge of childhood grief. You have demonstrated your desire to learn more just by picking up this book. While we will never evolve to a point of knowing "everything there is to know about death," we can always strive to broaden our understanding and degree of helpfulness. Take advantage of resources and training opportunities as they become available.

Another part of learning about grief involves exploring our assumptions about life and death. Think about your own personal losses. Who close to you has died? What did their deaths mean to you? Were you a child when someone you loved died? If so, how did you feel? How did the important adults in your life—including teachers and counselors—help you with your feelings of grief? Thinking about these issues will help you better help your students.

Teach what you learn to students

Don't wait until a student's parents are killed in a car accident to teach your class about death and grief. Make lesson plans that incorporate these important topics into the curriculum. And use natural, everyday encounters with death—a run-over squirrel, a death that made local headlines—to talk about your students' fears and concerns.

Remember the concepts of the "teachable moment," the "nurturing moment," and the "created moment."

- The ***teachable moment*** occurs when an opportunity to teach children about life and death arises through events happening around them. A baby is born; a classmate's grandfather dies. When these events occur, make positive use of them by talking openly about them with all the students.

- During ***nurturing moments***, you focus on the feelings of bereaved children. When a student's family member or friend or even pet dies, make yourself emotionally available to that student. Help him understand that mourning is a good thing and that he should feel safe to do it in your presence.

- Finally, the ***created moment*** means not waiting for "one big tell-all" about death but working to create regular opportunities to teach children about death. Children who have already been acquainted with the naturalness and permanence of death are more likely to grieve in healthy ways when someone they love dies.

How a grieving student might act

Behavioral problems

As covered in Chapter Three, many children express the pain of grief by acting out. This behavior varies depending on the child's age and developmental level. The child may become unusually loud and noisy, have a temper outburst, start fights with other children, defy authority, or simply rebel against everything. Other examples of acting-out behavior include getting poor grades or assuming a general attitude that says, "I don't care about anything." Older children may cut class or run away from home.

Underlying a grieving child's misbehavior are feelings of insecurity, abandonment, and low self-esteem. This basic recognition is the essence of artfully helping during this difficult time. My experience as a grief counselor has shown me that the two greatest needs of a grieving child are for affection and a sense of security. Appropriate limit-setting and discipline, then, should attempt to meet these essential needs. We must let bereaved students know that we care about them despite their present behavior.

Emotional symptoms

Grieving students will exhibit many of the thoughts and feelings discussed in Chapter Three. But peer pressure may sometimes force students to suppress these healthy thoughts and feelings during the school day. If, through a combination of education, modeling, and open communication, you can make your classroom a safe place for mourning, your bereaved students are more likely to share their grief with you and their classmates. And as we've said many times in this book, sharing our grief with others is an essential step toward healing.

Poor academic performance

Grief takes a physical, emotional, and spiritual toll on kids, and it may leave them feeling unable (or unwilling) to keep up with their schoolwork. Sometimes poor academic performance in a previously high-achieving student is a symptom that he needs more help with his grief, but sometimes bad grades or academic apathy are normal, temporary grief responses. Allow grieving children to concentrate on their grief first and their schoolwork second, at least for a while.

Getting extra help for the grieving student

When a student seems to be having a particularly hard time dealing with grief, help him get extra help. Explore the full spectrum of helping services in your community. Hospice bereavement programs, church groups, and private therapists are appropriate resources for some young people, while others may just need a little more time and attention from their parents or other caring adults.

If you decide that individual counseling outside the realm of school counseling might be able to help the bereaved student, try to find a counselor who specializes in bereavement counseling and has experience working with children. Search for counselors citing grief or bereavement as a specialty. Another credential to look for is certification from the Association for Death Education and Counseling.

Developing crisis response teams

For too many children, schools are no safe haven! The reality is that the rate of unexpected, violent deaths in adolescents in the United States has reached epidemic proportions. According to The Substance Abuse and Mental Health Services Administration (SAMHSA), homicide is the second leading cause of death (after unintended injuries such as motor vehicle crashes) for 15-24 year-olds, with suicide placing third.

Without a doubt, nothing can disrupt a school setting as quickly as the death of a member of that community. Fortunately, in the past couple of decades, school systems throughout North America have developed crisis response protocols that address tragic events. Crisis teams have been created to provide practical guidelines and staff when a tragic event impacts the school.

The formation of crisis response teams is now (in most circles) seen not just as a good idea, but a necessary responsibility. I have had the honor of helping a number of school systems establish these teams and training staff to respond in empathetic, supportive ways to students, staff and the community at large.

This section outlines some of the specifics that must be considered when you are establishing a crisis response team in the school setting. My hope is that this information will inspire schools that have not yet established such teams to move in that direction with haste.

Crisis response teams are created in an effort to:

- Provide a written protocol for the school system to respond when someone dies (whether that someone is a student, teacher, administrator, support staff or family member).

- Create a description of suggested qualifications and training requirements for people who make up the response team.

- Identify individual and group needs and create appropriate individual and group responses.

- Acknowledge the death and create an environment that allows for the need to mourn.

- Assist the people on the site of the death in responding meaningfully to those affected by the loss as well as meeting their own grief needs.

- Provide follow-up and referral services for people who will require and benefit from longer-term support.

Selection and preparation of staff team leaders

It is vitally important to carefully select those who will serve as team leaders. Do not assume that the training and education a school counselor, social worker, or psychologist has received has adequately prepared him to respond appropriately to the crisis of death. During graduate school many of these caregivers received only a very brief introduction ("Today we will cover death and grief") to bereavement care. The point is that those serving as crisis team leaders should demonstrate not only interest in this area, but the motivation to seek specialized training in grief counseling and crisis response work.

This training should:

- Explore personal loss issues and their place in one's life.

- Give a comprehensive understanding of the grief process, particularly as it relates to children and adolescents.

- Provide an in-depth understanding of the ways in which people naturally respond to traumatic death and the caregiver's subsequent helping roles.

- Share an overview of the collaborative-consulting role one will have when interacting with school administrators, teachers, support personnel, and families.

When a classmate dies

When a classmate dies, the other children will be profoundly impacted. They will probably feel a deep sense of loss and sadness, especially those who were among the classmate's close friends. Many will be curious. They will want to know what happened to Bobby and why. Some of the children will be afraid. When a classmate dies, children begin to understand that they, too, could die young.

Because the death was part of the children's school lives, teachers are the primary caregivers students look to for help with their grief. The first school day after the death (suspending classes for a day or two immediately following the death is sometimes a good idea), spend some class time explaining what happened. Remember to use simple, concrete language and honestly answer their questions. Model your own feelings. If you want to cry, cry—without apologizing for it. Later in the day you might have the children make drawings or write letters to give to the dead student's parents. Send a note home with students informing parents about the death. With parental permission, you might also arrange for interested students to attend the funeral. Holding an all-school memorial service is also often appropriate and healing. (The crisis response team model at the end of this chapter provides you and your fellow teachers and administrators a model for handling such news-breaking and follow-up more formally.)

And always remember, grief is a process, not an event. In the weeks and months to come, you will need to provide ongoing opportunities for your students to express their grief. Creating a photo or artwork display on a centrally-located bulletin board will help all the school's students acknowledge the reality of the death. Hang blank sheets of poster board throughout the school on which students can, whenever they feel moved to do so, jot down some thoughts and feelings about the death.

- Create an understanding of the various components that make up a school-based crisis response team.
- Assist in how to create teaching components for people who will make up the crisis response team.
- Promote an understanding of relevant ethical and legal issues.

Team members

Response team members can be drawn from the population of teachers, counselors, support staff and family members. From an ethical standpoint, I don't think anyone should be *forced* to serve on a crisis response team, even though for some staff members it may seem a natural fit given their job descriptions.

However, if you commit to a comprehensive training requirement for all team members, you can feel confident that almost anyone can be taught the necessary skills to serve on the team. What often cannot be taught is attitude. By allowing people to *volunteer* (rather than be recruited) for this special service, you will naturally select-in people who are open to learning about death, dying and loss issues. People not suitable for team members often drop out as they progress through the required training. This is at it should be.

Occasionally a team leader will have to supportively suggest that someone not be a member of the response team. This reality comes with the responsibility of being a team leader.

The training of team members is similar to the content of training outlined above for team leaders. The primary difference is that team leaders may seek even more training than team members, and, over time, become more experienced simply by virtue of the depth of experience.

Responsibility of administration and crisis team leaders

Administration

The school principal is usually the one in charge of the crisis response team at each individual school; however, we can use the word administrator here to indicate whoever is in the position of leadership in the school at the time of the death.

How the school as a community can acknowledge a death

When a student's family member or close friend dies, acknowledging the death is critical. Timeliness is important. Inform school personnel as well as the grieving student's classmates of the death and let them know the bereaved student will not be in school for at least several days.

The informing process should occur openly and be a vital part of other "news" that school personnel and students are made aware of. When the death is one that has impacted the entire school—death of a teacher, administrator, school support person, or student—everyone in the school should be properly informed. In those schools that have morning announcements through a public address system, I have found that this is an excellent opportunity to inform everyone at the same time. This should be done as soon as possible in that death news often travels fast and is often accompanied by false rumors. Let everyone know when the family is receiving friends at the funeral home, church or family home. Provide the date and time of the funeral service.

When a student's family member has died, peers of the student affected by the death should be encouraged to offer support to their classmate. A group letter from the class to the grieving student is often one of the most supportive gestures in the eyes of the child. I have worked with several classes where each student has written a personal note to the student. All of the notes were then placed in a tasteful box and delivered to the bereaved student by one of his better friends and/or the teacher.

The school counselor and teacher may want to decide together about the appropriateness of the child's classmates attending the funeral as a group. This opportunity can be offered and often provides the class with a sense of supporting their classmate. Be certain to obtain parental permission when doing this because (unfortunately) some parents will think attending a funeral is terribly inappropriate and harmful to their children.

In an effort to help classmates better understand what their peer is going through, I encourage teachers to ask others in the class who have experienced the death of someone close to them to talk about their experiences. Obviously, this serves as a model for the expression of concern for the recently grieving student and creates an atmosphere of openness surrounding the reality of death and grief. You might even talk to your students about ways of approaching and talking to the newly bereaved student when he returns to school. Help them understand that their classmate will still need friends and fun and that it's important they don't make him feel left out.

School-based peer support groups are another effective, healing forum for grieving kids. Many students are receptive to this and it aids them in feeling reintegrated into the school setting while at the same time acknowledging their grief. As many teachers and counselors know, bringing together a group of peers to express their thought and feelings creates a social network of support in which the students themselves can be most effective in helping each other. The *Companioning the Grieving Child Curriculum Book* contains a support group model and meeting plans designed to help you easily and effectively facilitate a support group for grieving kids and teens.

Helping Grieving Children at School Brochure
This information is also available in a brochure as a part of The Helping Series, a set of brochures for easy distribution to clients and families. Visit www.centerforloss.com and click on Brochures to order.

It is the administrator's job to:

- Contact the crisis response team leader when a death occurs.
- Schedule a meeting of the crisis response team in collaboration with the team leader.
- Arrange classroom coverage for any teacher team members.
- Prepare a memo to staff to communicate the facts surrounding the death or deaths.
- Arrange for informational notes to be sent home with students.
- Coordinate staff and student funeral attendance.
- Designate (when needed) a contact person for the media.

Crisis team leader

It is the crisis team leader's job to:

- Contact team members through a phone chain.
- Coordinate team response by providing leadership.
- Work with administration in gathering facts and preparing memos to staff and notes that go home with students.
- Assign team members and rooms to be used for crisis intervention and support.
- Assist in identifying primary survivors with special needs.
- Contact the family of the dead person to communicate support and provide assistance.
- Assist in the creation of meaningful rituals appropriate to the situation.
- Arrange for longer-term support systems (individual counseling, family counseling, support groups) to be available to those in need.

Implementation and communication plan

Take these steps to carry out a response to a death at school:

Anyone with initial knowledge of a death contacts the administrator

The administrator contacts the crisis response team leader

The team leader will contact team members

The administrator and team leader work to gather facts about
the death in preparation for initial team meeting

The meeting will be held as soon after the notification
of the event as possible

Response team meeting agenda

Administrator and team leader will give facts as known at this time

Team leader will outline plan of action

General outline for potential plan of action

To develop a plan of action, consider these items:

- Consider how and when death notification will occur.

- Assign team members to their individual responsibilities (e.g. who will go to what room to provide support).

- Coordinate communication with the family of the person who has died.

- Create awareness of who the primary survivors are.

- Review statement of procedure for any student who requests to go home.

- Review specific plan for remainder of the day in responding to the crisis.

- Team leader and administrator continue to monitor and supervise additional response team actions.

Follow-up considerations

Other considerations, when responding to a death, include:

- Plan for the inclusion of students and staff in the funeral or other mourning ritual (the school may decide to hold its own funeral or memorial service).

- Allow time after any funeral ritual for students to talk about the experience.

- Teach those who are impacted by the death (may include the entire school system) that healing in grief is a process, not an event.

- Create ways and means for students to give testimony to the life lived. For example: creating a scholarship in the name of the dead person, planting a tree, coordinating donations to family-specified organizations, writing a memorial for the yearbook.

- Provide ongoing grief support services and referrals to anyone in need.

- Assess the effectiveness of the crisis response team's efforts and revise the response protocol to make ongoing improvements.

- Schedule a structured follow-up assessment to be held three months from the tragic event to determine additional needs of survivors.

✳ ✳ ✳

While this chapter discussed how to support children at school, Chapter Eight describes the unique way teenagers grieve and the special care that's required to help them move through six distinct needs of mourning.

Chapter Eight

Companioning the Grieving Adolescent

Grieving adolescents remind me of a garden in June. They, too, can seem so exuberant, so autonomous, so mature, that they don't need our help—or certainly not as much help as younger children. Yet grieving teens do need our time and attention and vigilant understanding if they are to heal and grow into the autumn of their lives.

I've worked with hundreds of grieving adolescents, and they have taught me that, because of their already difficult life stage, their experience with grief is unique. They are not children, yet neither are they adults. Instead, teens constitute a special group of mourners who deserve a special kind of care and consideration from the adults around them.

Adolescent developmental tasks complicated by grief

With the exception of infancy, no developmental period is so filled with change as adolescence. One of the primary changes teenagers must go through is separating from their families. Leaving the security of childhood, adolescents begin to separate from their parents and siblings and establish their own identities. This process is very normal and necessary; without it, teens would never be able to leave home, establish careers or have families of their own.

But separating isn't always easy. With it comes the rebellion associated with adolescence. Fights with parents and siblings are common. So, when a parent or sibling who the teen has been at odds with dies, the teen may feel a sense of guilt or unfinished business.

Moreover, even though teens need to separate from their families, they still want to feel loved and secure. This ambivalence can complicate grief. The teen may think, "If I mourn, that means I need you. But my stronger need right now is for autonomy so I don't want to mourn."

As teenagers separate from their families, they attach more to their peer group. Friends, including love interests, may become the teen's most important source of affirmation and acceptance. So, if a teen's friend should die, the hurt can be particularly painful. And it can be difficult for grieving teens to turn to their parents for support when they are in the very process of separating from them. Finally, remember that for a teen, the death of a friend or sibling is the death of another young person. Not only will the teen probably feel despair and outrage at this injustice, but the death can also raise the frightening specter of the teen's own mortality.

Because early adolescence is often accompanied by awkward physical development, many teenagers feel unattractive. This can compromise their self-esteem and make them feel that much more overwhelmed by their grief. Adolescents' changing outward appearance can also make them look like men and women. Too often adults take this to mean that grieving teens are emotionally mature and can "handle" their own grief. Not so. No one, especially a young person, should have to cope with their grief alone. Grieving teenagers need the love and support of adults if they are to become emotionally healthy adults themselves.

School and sometimes jobs are also normal and necessary parts of the teenager's world. In fact, both help them hone their individuality and move toward independence. The death of someone loved, however, can put school and jobs on hold for a time. This, too, is normal. Grieving teens should not be asked to continue on with school and work as if nothing has happened. Actually, the work of mourning must take precedence if a teen is to heal. Parents, teachers, and other concerned adults should understand and even encourage this temporary shift in priorities. On the other hand, some teens channel their feelings of grief into their schoolwork. These young people may see their grades or job performance go *up*.

One last point here is that teens, like children, often do "catch-up" mourning at developmental milestones. Important events like prom or high school graduation may cause the bereaved teen to feel particularly sad because the person who died isn't there to share that moment. This occurrence is normal not only shortly after the death of someone loved, but also years later. In fact, many grieving teens will continue to do catch-up mourning as they enter adulthood and reach other milestones like marrying or having children.

Nature of the death

In Chapter Two we explored at some length how the nature of the death can influence a child's grief journey. Here I would like to revisit this important topic *as it applies to teenagers.*

For many teens, the first special person in their life to die is a grandparent. If the teen was close to Grandma or Grandpa, this death can be a very significant loss in the teen's life and should be recognized as such. Too often the teen will hear others say, "She was very old and sick anyway," or, "He lived a long, full life." The fact that the grandparent was old does not take away the teen's right to mourn.

The death of a pet can also be very painful for adolescents. Sometimes they have grown up with the pet and have spent years caring for it, playing and sleeping with it. Teens who have emotionally distanced themselves from family members may actually be *more* bonded to the pet than they are to people. As a caring adult, you can validate the teen's need to mourn this loss.

Most of the other deaths that teens experience are sudden or untimely. A parent may die of a heart attack, a brother or sister may die of cancer, or a friend may complete suicide or be killed in a car accident. The very nature of these deaths often causes the teen to feel a prolonged and heightened sense of unreality.

At first, the teen will often feel disbelief and numbness. His survival mechanisms tell him that he must push away this horrible reality if he is to survive. Fear, panic, and withdrawal are also common responses to sudden death. The teen may worry that someone else close to her, or even she herself, will die, too.

The adolescent's heightened emotions often take the form of rage after a sudden death. Anger is a way for the teen to say, "I protest this death" and to vent her feelings of helplessness.

Rage fantasies are also common. For example, if a teen's mom was killed in a car crash, the teen may express a desire to murder the drunk driver at fault. Try not to be frightened by this rage. It is a normal grief response, and most teens know not to act upon these feelings. However, some will need help in exploring the distinction between feeling rage and taking action.

If someone loved dies after a long illness, keep in mind that the teen probably began the grief process (often called anticipatory grief) long before the actual death. The teen's need to push away painful realities is stronger than an adult's, so they sometimes feel a greater sense of shock and numbness when the person who has been ill dies. Young people who have had accurate information about the terminal illness withheld from them are also likely to feel shocked when the person dies. Finally, understand that after the long illness of someone they love, teens may feel a sense of relief. This, too, is normal and in no way equals a lack of love for the person who died.

The death of a parent can be especially difficult for all young people. Teenagers look to the future more than younger children do, and expect their parents to grow old and be grandparents to the children they may eventually have. A parent's premature death, then, is the death of the teen's dreams for the future.

As we have already said, teens can also be extremely close to boyfriends, girlfriends, and best friends. If one of these important people should die, teens need the opportunity to mourn. Unfortunately, their grief is not always acknowledged because society tends to focus on the "primary" mourners: the dead person's immediate family.

The grieving teen's support systems

Many people assume that the grieving adolescent's friends and family members will support them in their grief journeys. In reality, this may not be true at all.

First of all, the teen's surviving parent or siblings may not be able to offer support because they are so overwhelmed by their own grief. This is natural and shouldn't be considered selfish or wrong, but it does mean that the teen will need extra support and caring from non-family members during this difficult time.

The grieving teen's lack of support may also relate to the social expectations placed on the young person. Teens are usually expected to be "grown up" and support other members of the family, particularly a surviving parent or younger brothers and sisters. Many teens have been told, "Now you will have to take care of your family." The problem is this: When a teenager feels responsible for "taking care of the family," she doesn't have the opportunity, or the permission, to mourn.

Sometimes we assume that teenagers will find comfort from their peers. When it comes to death, this may not be true, either. Many bereaved teens are actually greeted with indifference by their peers. It seems that unless their friends have experienced grief themselves, they project their feelings of helplessness by ignoring the subject of loss entirely. Worse yet, some of the teenager's peers may be insensitive or even cruel. It's not unusual to see peers avoid the grieving teen out of an unconscious fear that death might become a part of their lives, as well. Or, sometimes peers try to force the grieving teen to avoid the pain of grief and just get on with life. I call this "buck-up therapy." Teens seem to be more comfortable sharing the good times. You can help by teaching teens what being a good friend in grief means.

The adolescent's mourning needs

In Chapter Four we explored in depth the six reconciliation needs of mourning, particularly as they applied to younger children. But how are those needs made unique by adolescence?

Need 1: Acknowledge the reality of the death.

Teenagers are not immune from magical thinking. They will sometimes fuel their guilt about the death by literally blaming themselves if they are not helped to reframe this common but devastating feeling. For example, you might hear a teen say, "If I hadn't goofed off so much and made her worry, my Mom wouldn't have gotten so sick." To be helpful, you must respect the teen's need to express these "if-onlys," but over time help her come to understand the limits of her own culpability.

Need 2: Move toward the pain of the loss.

Keep in mind that teens' naturally strong resistance to mourning does not mean that they are not hurting inside or that they are incapable of mourning when given support and understanding. Also remember that because teens don't always articulate their feelings well, they often do as much if not more of their mourning through their behaviors rather than words.

You can help by redirecting inappropriate behaviors. Let bereaved teens know that it's OK to feel angry but that it's not OK to physically hurt themselves or others because of this anger. Find an appropriate way for the angry teen to release his explosive emotions.

Before teens will open up to you, though, you must show them that you care and understand. You can best earn this trust by entering the teen's world first and counseling second. Don't always take teenagers to your office. Instead, shoot baskets with them or go out for a cheeseburger. During these activities, mix small talk with serious talk.

Need 3: Remember the person who died

As you help grieving teens through their grief journeys, be alert for creative and spontaneous ways to remember the person who died. Journal writing can be particularly effective for adolescents who may not be ready yet to talk openly about their feelings. When words are inadequate, group rituals like planting a tree or dedicating a plaque can be helpful. They also provide concrete memorials that the teens can revisit long into the future. Finally, keep in mind that remembering can be difficult for teens. Some memories are painful, even frightening. But many are joyful and allow the teen to relive the happy times. With your help, grieving adolescents can discover the beauty of memory: through it, the person who died can live on inside them forever.

Need 4: Develop a new self-identity

As social beings, we think of ourselves in relation to the people around us. I'm not just Alan Wolfelt, but a son, a brother, a husband, a friend. Teenagers may be even more closely linked to those around them than adults are because their self-identities are just emerging. So, when someone loved dies, teens must begin the difficult process of forming an identity apart from that person.

We should never assign inappropriate roles to young people, especially those that force them prematurely into adulthood. For example, teen boys should not be pressured to financially support their families like dad did. Nor should teen girls have to take the place of mom. This type of role substitution is both unhealthy and unfair to bereaved teenagers. Emotional role changing is equally damaging. For instance, if a teen's father dies, the mother should not rely on the teen for the emotional support her husband once gave her.

The grieving teen's identity is also affected by the realization that he will experience losses in life. Some young people may temporarily evolve a more serious or cautious view of themselves and the world that reflects this vulnerability. Sometimes this seriousness develops as the grieving teen searches for meaning and often lightens as the grieving process unfolds. As caregivers, we must be watchful that this seriousness does not prevent the teen from having fun and does not develop into chronic depression.

Need 5: Search for meaning

Grieving young people naturally ask "how" and "why" questions about the death of someone loved. We can help by letting the bereaved teen know that these kinds of questions are both normal and important. Remember, normalize but don't minimize.

You should also note that teenagers sometimes act out their search for meaning. Drunk driving and other behaviors that test their mortality are common. While in general you shouldn't judge the ways in which the grieving young person searches for meaning, life-threatening behaviors obviously require intervention.

Need 6: Continue to receive support from adults.

Grief is a process, not an event, and like all of us, grieving adolescents will continue to need the support of helping adults long after the death.

Signs a teen may need extra help

As we have discussed, there are many reasons why healthy grieving can be especially difficult for adolescents. Not only are the deaths encountered by teens often sudden and unexpected, but their lives may be filled with emotional turmoil anyway. Being a teenager is hard enough; being a bereaved teenager can be overwhelming.

Just like any bereaved person, grieving teens need the help and support of those around them if they are to heal. Sometimes, though, grieving adolescents need extra help.

But how do you tell if teens need extra help reconciling their grief? First, don't get caught up in trying to determine which behaviors can be attributed to normal adolescent struggles and which have been precipitated by the death of someone loved. The work of adolescent development and the work of grief are alike in that they both involve mourning losses and accepting changes. Trying to separate them is beside the point.

To determine if the bereaved teen needs extra help, it is more important for you to distinguish between normal behaviors—no matter their cause—and dangerous behaviors. Following are lists of both normal behaviors and those that should be considered "red flags"—warning signs that the grieving teen is having serious problems that warrant professional attention.

Normal behaviors

- Some limit-testing and rebellion
- Increased reliance on peers (vs. parents) for support and problem solving
- Egocentrism
- Increased moodiness
- Increased sexual awareness
- Impulsiveness, lack of common sense

Teens will be teens, and many of the ways in which they try adults' patience are perfectly normal. Of course, grieving teens are no different; they will exhibit these behaviors, too. Expect some limit-testing and rebellion, like staying out past curfew or arguing with parents. Adolescents also show an increased reliance on their peers for support and problem solving. Egocentrism is normal, too. Young people think the world revolves around them, and they sometimes fulfill their own needs at the expense of others. Teens are also moody. Don't be alarmed by their see-sawing emotions. Of course, adolescence is by definition a period of physical change and increased sexual awareness. At times the teen may seem to think of little else. Finally, young people can be impulsive and may seem to lack common sense.

"Red flag" behaviors

- Suicidal thoughts or actions
- Chronic depression, sleeping difficulties, and low self esteem
- Isolation from family and friends
- Academic failure or overachievement
- Dramatic change in personality or attitude
- Eating disorders
- Drug and alcohol abuse
- Fighting or legal troubles
- Inappropriate sexual behaviors

Because teens are going through a developmentally difficult time, we need to give them some leeway. Their frustrating actions are often normal, as we have just pointed out. But adolescents—grieving adolescents, especially—may also exhibit behaviors that are not normal and should be stopped. Suicidal thoughts or actions, such as giving away personal belongings or threatening suicide, are obviously a cry for help and should be taken very seriously. Chronic depression, sleeping difficulties, and low self-esteem are also signs that a grieving teen needs extra help. Isolation from family and friends is another red flag behavior. While teens need to emotionally distance themselves from their parents, they should not physically shut themselves in their rooms and prevent all interaction.

Abandoning friends, those all-important people in the young person's life, is definitely a signal that something is wrong. Academic failure can also be a cry for help. As we have said, it's important to let teens mourn first and concentrate on school second. But a total loss of interest in academics, especially for a prolonged period, can signify trouble. (On the other hand, focusing on school to the exclusion of all else, especially the necessary work of mourning, can be a warning sign, too.) You should also look for a dramatic change in personality or attitude. Like everyone, teens are changed forever when someone loved dies, but they should not act like an entirely different person.

Eating disorders are another common manifestation of complicated grief. Be on the watch for symptoms of anorexia or bulimia. Finally, risk-taking such as drug or alcohol abuse, fighting, legal troubles and sexual promiscuity should not be tolerated. Grieving teens sometimes behave in these ways to prove their own invincibility. But no matter the impetus, these actions can harm the teen or others and should be stopped.

As with any checklist, the above lists are not all-inclusive nor are they meant to replace an in-depth assessment by a trained professional. They should, however, help you begin to understand what constitutes a "cry for help" on the part of the bereaved teen. Any behavior that may harm the teen or another person requires immediate intervention. Short of that, be on the watch for severe and prolonged bouts of unhappiness, anger, or even indifference.

Also be aware that adolescents who have experienced multiple losses, such as having several friends die in a single car accident or losing a grandparent and shortly thereafter a parent, are probably more at risk for complicated grief. Grieving teens already dealing with a family problem like alcoholism or abuse will also likely need extra help. These young people, especially, need care and support if they are to heal.

If you think a bereaved teen might need extra help, explore the full spectrum of helping services in your community. Hospice bereavement programs, school counselors, church groups, and private therapists are appropriate resources for some young people, while others may just need a little more time and attention from their parents or other caring adults.

Support groups comprised of other teens who have experienced the loss of someone loved can also be a great resource. In these groups, teens can share their unique grief journeys in a nonthreatening, safe atmosphere. And, while the grieving teen's friends may feel unable to help because they haven't experienced such a loss, support group members offer both compassion and peer support. (The *Companioning the Grieving Child Curriculum Book* contains a support group model and meeting plans designed to help you easily and effectively facilitate a support group for grieving kids and teens.)

Finally, remember that finding a counselor or support group for the bereaved teen is one thing; hospitalizing him or her is another. Inpatient mental health care can be very beneficial to bereaved people who need to immerse themselves in intensive, around-the-clock grief work to heal. But less restrictive therapy options, like outpatient counseling and support groups, should always be considered first. Many professionals feel that hospitalization is overused, especially for teenagers, and the costs can be astronomical. If you're in doubt about hospitalizing a grieving teen, I recommend you consult professionals with expertise in this area.

Teen Grief Realities

The following statements and follow-up implications are based on my counseling experiences with hundreds of teens. Some are consistent with research, others are simply my subjective observations. Use what is helpful; discard what is not.

1. 1. Many teens have a great resistance to counseling and/or support groups.
   Implication: We must be outreach-oriented in our helping efforts.

2. Several studies have found that a teen's reconciliation of a death is a function of family system issues, and many parents of today's teens grew up in a mourning-avoiding culture.
   Implication: Family systems must be a focus.

3. A differential response has been found between male and female teens. Males tend to have a more aggressive grief response. They may act out physically or use drugs or alcohol. Females in contrast often feel a longing for comfort and reassurance.
   Implication: Be aware of and responsive to these differences.

4. Teens mourn in doses.
   Implication: They need permission to not always be openly mourning. Some teens may need some distractions or "time-outs" from more active mourning. In contrast, others may benefit from encouragement to create "mourning times" or they could get caught up in distractions.

5. While it is important for healthy mourning that adolescents be able to openly express feelings, they may not do so if it sets them apart from their peers.
   Implications: Create opportunities for peer support from teens who have "been there."

6. In times of ongoing stress, many teens report a need for some privacy or "alone time."
   Implication: Don't be threatened by this while at the same time staying available to the teen.

7. Many teens fear loss of emotional control and may be frightened by normal feelings of grief.
   Implication: To help prevent the "going crazy syndrome," we need to help grieving teens understand the multitude of thoughts and feelings they may have. Teens need to know that sleep dis-

*turbances, appetite changes, anxiety and fears, irritability, explo-
sive emotions etc. are all common responses to death.*

8. Most teens are unfamiliar with the intensity and the duration of
   grief responses.
   *Implication: Teens need to know that grief is a process, not an
   event. The pace of healing will be unique to each person. They
   need a realistic timeframe for doing the work of mourning. They
   may be surrounded by adults who are impatient with them and
   project they should "be back to normal" quickly and efficiently.*

9. Shy, quiet teens will naturally have a more difficult time expressing their grief in words.
   *Implication: Nonverbal teens may need support in accessing
   nonverbal means of expressing their grief. Art, music, and journ-
   aling may be more appropriate avenues of expression than talking for these teens. But watch closely: These teens are easy to
   miss because they are more withdrawn.*

10. Some teens invite adults into defensive interactions (usually
    through expressing hostility and a sense that "no one understands
    or cares about me") that serve to distract everyone from the under-
    lying pain of the loss.
    *Implication: Recognize that in companioning bereaved teens
    you may be a whipping post for some who are likely to express
    their underlying pain through anger. The key is to not get
    involved in a defensive interaction that might cause you to miss
    the communication about underlying feelings of helplessness.
    Appropriate behavioral limits need to be set while the underlying
    pain is explored and expressed.*

A FINAL WORD

"A child needs encouragement like a plant needs water."
—Rudolph Dreikurs, M.D.

The opportunity to companion grieving children is a privilege that has allowed me to be drawn more fully into the richness and beauty of life. Bereaved children, having experienced the death of someone loved, must explore how they will go on to live their own lives and how they will relate to people and the world around them. As a companion, I have been changed in powerful ways impossible to capture in words. To grief garden for me is to embrace what is good, honest, and beautiful.

Companioning children is helped by compassionate curiosity. When we take off our professional masks and create sacred, hospitable free space for the mourner, we allow them to grow at their own pace and in their own way. Compassionate curiosity encourages us to extend ourselves rather than withdraw into our own worlds. We are invited to open our hearts wide, be still, and really listen with all of our senses.

I hope that the companioning and grief-gardening model has inspired and challenged you. Over the years, it has certainly challenged me and ultimately increased my flexibility as a caregiver. If this book encourages you to be a more open companion to grieving kids, I'm thankful. In sharing my ideas I hope I have engaged your minds and your hearts. For it is in transforming our thinking through learning that we transform our lives and the lives of those we hope to help.

My Grief Rights

A Handout for Grieving Kids

Someone you love has died. You are probably having many hurtful and scary thoughts and feelings right now. Together those thoughts and feelings are called grief, which is a normal, though really difficult, thing everyone goes through after someone they love has died.

The following ten rights will help you understand your grief and eventually feel better about life again. Use the ideas that make sense to you. Post this list on your refrigerator or on your bedroom wall. Re-reading it often will help you stay on track as you move toward healing from your loss. You might also ask the grown-ups in your life to read this list so they will remember to help you in the best way they can.

1. **I have the right to have my own unique feelings about the death.** I may feel mad, sad, or lonely. I may feel scared or relieved. I may feel numb or sometimes not anything at all. No one will feel exactly like I do.

2. **I have the right to talk about my grief whenever I feel like talking.** When I need to talk, I will find someone who will listen to me and love me. When I don't want to talk about it, that's OK, too.

3. **I have the right to show my feelings of grief in my own way.** When they are hurting, some kids like to play so they'll feel better for a while. I can play or laugh, too. I might also get mad and scream. This does not mean I am bad, it just means I have scary feelings that I need help with.

4. **I have the right to need other people to help me with my grief, especially grown-ups who care about me.** Mostly I need them to pay attention to what I am feeling and saying and to love me no matter what.

5. **I have the right to get upset about normal, everyday problems**. I might feel grumpy and have trouble getting along with others sometimes.

YOU MIGHT ALSO LIKE...

The Companioning the Grieving Child Curriculum Book

Activities to Help Children and Teens Heal

By Patricia Morrissey, M.S. Ed.
Foreword by Alan D. Wolfelt, Ph.D.

Softcover • 208 pages • $29.95
ISBN 978-1-617221-85-9
Published October 2012

Based on Dr. Wolfelt's six needs of mourning and written to pair with *Companioning the Grieving Child*, this comprehensive guide provides hundreds of hands-on activities tailored for grieving children in three age groups: preschool, elementary, and teens. Through the use of readings, games, discussion questions, and arts and crafts, counselors will help grieving young people acknowledge the reality of the death, embrace the pain of the loss, remember the person who died, develop a new self-identity, search for meaning, and accept support from others.

Sample activities include:

• Grief sock puppets

• Tissue paper butterflies in conjunction with the picture book *My, Oh My—A Butterfly!*

• Expression bead bracelets

• The nurturing game

• Write an autobiopoem

Throughout the book, the theme of butterflies reminds readers that just as butterflies go through metamorphosis, so do grieving children. Activities are in an easy-to-follow format, each with a goal, objective, sequential description of the activity, and a list of needed materials.

6. **I have the right to have "griefbursts."** Griefbursts are sudden, unexpected feelings of sadness that just hit me sometimes—even long after the death. These feelings can be very strong and even scary. When this happens, I might feel afraid to be alone.
7. **I have the right to use my beliefs about my god to help me deal with my feelings of grief.** Praying might make me feel better and somehow closer to the person who died.
8. **I have the right to try to figure out why the person I loved died.** But it's OK if I don't find an answer. "Why" questions about life and death are the hardest questions in the world.
9. **I have the right to think and talk about my memories of the person who died.** Sometimes those memories will be happy and sometimes they might be sad. Either way, these memories help me keep alive my love for the person who died.
10. **I have the right to move toward and feel my grief, and, over time, to heal.** I'll go on to live a happy life, but the life and death of the person who died will always be a part of me. I will always miss them.

My Grief Rights Poster
This information is also available in a 4-color, 24" by 36" poster. The contemporary design and straightforward-but-non-condescending text also make it appropriate for grieving teenagers. Visit www.centerforloss.com and click on Posters to order.

Additional Materials on Grieving Teens and Children by this Author

Besides this book, Dr. Wolfelt has created a variety of materials on children's grief. These items include books, posters, brochures, and wallet cards that can be used for personal reference, display items in your office, or as easy hand-outs to families and clients. For more information, visit the bookstore at centerforloss.com and click on "For and About Grieving Teens and Children" for a complete list.